Entertaining in Style

A year of recipes, menus & celebrations

5124 Entertaining in Style
Published in 1999 by CLB
© 1999 Quadrillion Publishing Ltd
Godalming Business Centre
Woolsack Way, Godalming
Surrey, England GU7 1XW

Distributed in the USA by
Quadrillion Publishing, Inc.
230 Fifth Avenue
New York, NY 10001

ISBN 1-84100-068-X

Printed at Oriental Press, Dubai, U.A.E.

Design
Paul Turner and Sue Pressley,
    Stonecastle Graphics Ltd, Marden, Kent
Additional craft items by Julie Davies

Photography
Paul Turner and Sue Pressley
Neil Sutherland
Peter Barry

Editorial
Compiled and written by Wendy Hobson
American adaptation by Josephine Bacon
Edited by Joseph F Ryan

Director of Production
Graeme Procter

Entertaining in Style

A year of recipes, menus & celebrations

Compiled and written by Wendy Hobson

CLB

The delights of entertaining

Whether in the simplest of settings or at the most lavish dinner party, sharing food has always been an expression of friendship. The host or hostess gladly accepts the responsibility for making guests welcome and serving them the best food, beautifully presented, in a congenial atmosphere.

Sounds simple? Of course! Until you plan your party and don't know where to start, or run out of ideas on how to make your party or celebration different from any other. Everyone needs a source of new ideas—special ways of arranging flowers for the table, different and interesting recipes, unusual gifts for guests—to make their parties stand out from the crowd.

This book is packed with the information you need to help you make your entertaining more stylish, more stunning, more fun! It will give you all sorts of ideas on every aspect of entertaining—from etiquette and presentation to floral arrangements and drinks.

Choosing a theme

So where do you start? You have decided on the occasion. You know where, when, and whom to invite. What do you do next?

One of the best ways to help you in your planning is to set a theme for your occasion. Some events will set their own style—a wedding, a christening, a special anniversary. Use that to give you ideas to link together the menu you choose and how you present it. Perhaps it is a silver wedding anniversary, for example. Use plain white china with a silver decoration, or serve your meal on silver platters; pick silver leaves with white or a startling contrast in flowers for your table decorations, or choose dried arrangements sprayed with silver; write your place cards in silver ink or construct them in silver paper; wrap little gifts of candy in silver cones with trailing silver ribbons.

If the occasion does not have a particular theme—perhaps it is just a dinner party for friends—there are always ways of directing your thoughts to give you exciting and inventive ideas, and one of the best ways is to think about the seasons. To start with, the seasons themselves can give you ideas—light and simple buffets for spring, barbecues for balmy summer nights, warming suppers for fall evenings or rich, old-fashioned fare for winter get-togethers with friends. Colors, too, come to mind—the yellows of spring, the multicolors of summer, russets of fall, and black-and-white of winter.

There is never a shortage of seasonal events to use as a theme for your celebration. You will have your own list of birthdays and anniversaries to celebrate, but there are plenty of other ready-made excuses—should you need one—for inviting friends to share your hospitality. Saints' days, Easter, Passover, Thanksgiving right through to Christmas—anything can be chosen to give structure and coherence to your plans.

And why not be international or look to other cultures for your ideas? Especially if you have recently returned from a vacation, you will be in a perfect position to startle and delight your friends with cuisine with an international flavor—perhaps Italian-style wines served with Mediterranean fare on a cloth of white with green and red napkins; or exuberant red, white, and blue with blueberry pie and English muffins for a Fourth of July afternoon tea in the garden!

Party planning

No matter how large or small your gathering, the better you plan it in advance, the more you will enjoy it, and the happier your guests will be. Inviting the neighbors round for an impromptu glass of wine may be great fun, but if you have planned an occasion, you will want to do something a little more special.

Thinking ahead

It is a good idea to keep a notebook and record your party plans. It helps to ensure that nothing is forgotten—and you can double-check that you do not offer a similar meal to the same guests when you invite them again!

So, firstly, list the guests you plan to invite and ask yourself a few questions. Do you have enough for the kind of event you envisage? Do you have too many and need to cut down or change your plans? A lively dancing party may not get off the ground with only a dozen people, but with more than eight at a dinner party, you will find that it is not easy to hold a single conversation and people will divide into groups. Will your guests enjoy each other's company? What special needs do they have—are any vegan, vegetarian, or with other dietary needs?

You can telephone friends to invite them, but a formal occasion requires written invitations, sent out between ten days and three weeks beforehand so that guests have time to make their arrangements, book babysitters, and so on. You should give the arrival time on the invitation, 8 p.m. for 8:30 p.m., for example, and indicate if it is a formal occasion and special dress is required. Guests should respond straight away so that you can avoid making last-minute invitations to make up numbers. If you do have to do that, ask some close friends to whom you can explain the situation and who know that they are frequently invited in their own right!

Next think about the logistics of the party. Is it a formal meal or a buffet? Do you have enough chairs? What about china, flatware, glasses, linen and napkins, ashtrays? If you consider these aspects in good time, you can easily buy, borrow, or hire to suit the occasion. Bear in mind that, for a buffet party, you will always need more glasses than there are guests, so take advantage of any free hire offers in liquor stores.

What about presentation? Will you prepare your own flower arrangements or decorations, or do you have a willing friend who will conjure up some wonderful displays in return for a favor? Would you rather buy something from a florist or display your new candelabra? Have you practiced that special napkin fold? What about lighting to create the atmosphere you want—subtle, but not gloomy? What about music? And, for a barbecue or outdoor event, what will you do if it pours with rain?

The food, of course, is the central pivot of the event. Take your time to select the perfect menu which your guests will savor and which you will be proud to serve. Start by deciding how many courses or dishes you will serve, then choose the entrée first, working outward from that to achieve a menu that balances light courses with rich, is varied but with each course complementing the next, and is not too complicated—trying something fancy which you have never made before is a recipe for disaster. If you want to serve something new and different, have a trial run with your family. Since most people now have a freezer, you may like to choose some courses that can be made in advance, and this is certainly a good idea for a large buffet. Don't choose dishes that need last-minute preparation or can easily fail—unless you are an excellent cook, forget the soufflé! If one or two courses can be prepared in advance and served cold, then you will have more time to enjoy the company of your guests.

Plan the drinks, too. If you are serving wines, choose wines to complement the food, not to fight with it. And always, remember that at most parties at least one person will have to drive home. Make sure you have nonalcoholic drinks that are as pleasant to enjoy as your wines, or you will feel embarrassed at having nothing more interesting to offer your guests than a can of soda pop with their bœuf en croûte!

Entertaining etiquette

The formal dinner party reached its zenith in the early 1900s, when the hostess really needed to be mistress of the fine art of etiquette. At formal occasions, escorts, seating arrangements, order of serving, everything was carried out strictly by the rank of the guests—and a social *gaffe* would not quickly be forgotten!

Fortunately for the modern hostess, things are much more relaxed now, and you are unlikely to have to work out whether a naval captain should sit higher up the table than a colonel! The most important considerations of etiquette today relate to courtesy and the comfort of your guests. However, this is often best achieved by following the basic rules of etiquette.

Seating arrangements

Formally, the host and hostess sit at either end of the table, with the highest ranking guests sitting nearest to the host, usually alternating male and female guests, with partners sitting opposite one another. A guest of honor should sit next to the host. Otherwise, common interests are more relevant than rank in deciding where to place your guests.

Laying the table

Most modern dinner parties offer three courses, and this is quite sufficient for most occasions. You probably will not have enough china and flatware to offer the traditional nine courses: soup, fish, sherbet, entrée, salad, dessert, savory dish, cheese, and fruit.

For a formal occasion linen should be white, but if you have a beautiful table you may prefer to use place mats with white or colored napkins. A decorative table centerpiece, perhaps with candles, is an attractive starting point, but remember that your guests will want to talk to each other, so don't make it too tall. Handwritten place cards—giving the full name for a formal party—should be in place before the diners are asked to take their places. Butter, salt and pepper, and mustard if suitable, should also be on the table. Pepper mills are not traditionally used, but since freshly ground pepper tastes vastly superior, many people are now ignoring this "rule."

Left: Presentation is vital to successful entertaining. Here, highly polished silverware, china, and glasses, with lovely linen and flowers, combine to create an atmosphere of opulence and welcome.

Above: A formal table setting for dinner. Traditional candlesticks provide a touch of distinction for any occasion, and the glimmer of soft candlelight will set the mood for an elegant evening of entertainment.

China and serving dishes for a formal table setting should all match and you should provide everything the diner needs for all the courses you are intending to serve, including separate plates for salad and cheese, if they are included on the menu. Any course served in a bowl should have a separate plate underneath the bowl.

Silverware should also be matching. Knives and spoons are placed on the right of the plate, blades inward, forks on the left, to be used from the outside working in toward the center. For less formal occasions, dessert spoons and forks can be placed above the table setting.

You should provide a suitable wine glass for each wine to be served. Place the glasses to the diners' right in the order in which they will be used, working from right to left, or left to right, or in a triangular pattern. Port or liqueur glasses are brought in after the meal with the drinks.

Choosing wines

Your choice of wines will depend on the occasion, but aim to find a style of wine appropriate to your kind of party. If you are not knowledgeable about wine, ask advice at a good liquor store. Explain the occasion and show the manager the menu, indicate your budget and the quantities you require, and he or she should be only too pleased to give you good advice.

Here are a few pointers to help you choose suitable wines every time:

- Aperitifs should stimulate the appetite, so a light wine or a dry sherry are good choices. Avoid very sweet or heavy drinks.

- Light wines are best with light foods.

- Serve white wines before red, and dry wines before sweet.

- If a wine has been used in a dish, it is a good wine to serve with that dish.

- Wines from a particular region usually go well with food from the same region.

- Fish is usually partnered by dry white wines. Red wines can taste metallic.

- Rich meat and game dishes should be served with a full-bodied red wine. Other red meats can be served with a lighter red wine.

- White meat is usually served with a medium-dry white wine, but it can also be served with a light red.

- If you are serving just one wine with the meal, select a light wine that will complement the whole meal.

- Cheeses go best with red wine or port.

- Desserts should be served with champagne or a sweet dessert wine.

One bottle of wine yields about six glasses; allow half to three-quarters of a bottle for each guest.

Serve wine at the temperature which shows off its best characteristics. Sparkling wines and white wines are generally served chilled, red wines at room temperature. Open red wines an hour or so before the meal.

Only vintage wines and ports really need to be decanted, leaving the sediment behind in the bottle. If you are lucky enough to be able to serve these, decant them by holding the bottle over a light and pouring the wine very slowly into the decanter, stopping as the sediment nears the neck.

Serving food and wine

Food should be served from the left-hand side of guests. The formal order of serving at a dinner party is to start with the woman on the host's right and move clockwise around the table, and if you have someone to serve the meal, or the host and hostess are serving their guests, you should follow this sequence. If guests are helping themselves, the hostess should pass the serving dish to the guest on her right, who will pass the plate anti-clockwise around the table.

Formally, a finger bowl is offered to each guest after the entrée on a dessert plate with a dessert knife and fork on either side.

Wine is served from the right, then passed to the left. Glasses should be filled two-thirds full to allow the guests to savor the bouquet of the wine. On very formal occasions, keep the wine on the sideboard so that a wine waiter can top up the guests' glasses during the meal. Normally, however, it is perfectly acceptable to leave the wine on the table, usually to be poured by the host although you may like to invite your guests to help themselves.

After the meal

The table is generally cleared before the dessert course, but if the hostess is doing all the work it can be left to her discretion.

Smoking is not polite until after all the eating has been completed, and you may like to signal this by placing a few ashtrays on the table when the meal is finished.

Coffee and liqueurs can be served at the table, or you can withdraw to the lounge, closing the door on all the clearing up to be done. If you remain at the table, it is quite polite for guests to move seats to talk to other guests, and you can take the lead by doing this first.

January

A new year of entertaining is under way and your resolution can be to achieve the style and sophistication you have admired as other people's guest. Be confident in your own abilities and you will find that you, too, can entertain with flair and panache.

A dinner party table

This simple Greek salad looks exquisite on a beautifully presented table, illustrating the importance of style, color-matching, and presentation. Subtlety, exuberance, celebration—capture the atmosphere you want by your table setting.

Linen should be crisp and spotlessly clean, or if you have a beautiful table you may opt for place-mats, as in this sophisticated combination of embroidered cutwork with crochet.

China, silverware, and glassware should be matching. If you do not have a dinner service, try borrowing from a friend. Those who entertain regularly will want to build up a classic service—perhaps a few pieces at a time. If your budget is tight, keep to simple white china and stylish but inexpensive glassware.

A simple yet bright floral decoration is a welcoming sight for your guests as they arrive.

1 New Year's Day

2

3

4

Warm brandy snaps then shape them into baskets to fill with fruit or ice cream.

Chocolate-rum meringues

4 egg whites
pinch of salt
1 cup superfine sugar
2 oz butter
1 cup confectioners' sugar
1 egg yolk
4 squares semi-sweet
  baking chocolate
1 tbsp dark rum

Whip the egg
whites and salt until
stiff but not dry. Add 2 tbsp
superfine sugar and whisk until stiff and shiny. Fold in the
remaining sugar. Drop spoonfuls onto cookie sheets lined with
nonstick baking paper and bake in a preheated oven at 250°F
for 2 hours or until dry. Beat the butter and confectioners'
sugar until fluffy then beat in the egg yolk. Melt the chocolate
with the rum, then beat it into the buttercream. Fill the
meringues and garnish with chocolate curls.

Butterfly napkins

Fold two edges to meet in the
center then fold over in half.
Double-fold the sides to the
center. Pull the right-hand
back corner to the left to make
a triangle, fold back and repeat
on the other side.

5

*Use white linen for a formal
dinner, but have fun color-
matching on more relaxed
evenings.*

6

7

*A wine cooler is a good way of
keeping white wines at serving
temperature.*

Children's party penguin

An elaborate flower arrangement would not be especially appreciated at a children's party. Instead, experiment with some paper folding or sculpture or make a fun table centerpiece—or use a Christmas decoration. If you are good at handicrafts, there are plenty of great books in the libraries and bookstores which will give you ideas for table centerpieces such as this cute little party penguin. If you fear that all the children would want to take him home, make something a little less ambitious so that you can sit one on each plate. If crafts are not your style, make a display of some toys to brighten the center of the table.

Mix spoonfuls of popcorn and unsalted roasted peanuts in buttered patty pans. Dissolve 1½ cups sugar in ½ cup water and boil for 10 minutes, or until golden. Pour over the popcorn and leave to set.

8

9

10

Preplanning is vital to ensure that you are always in control and keeping the children busy.

11

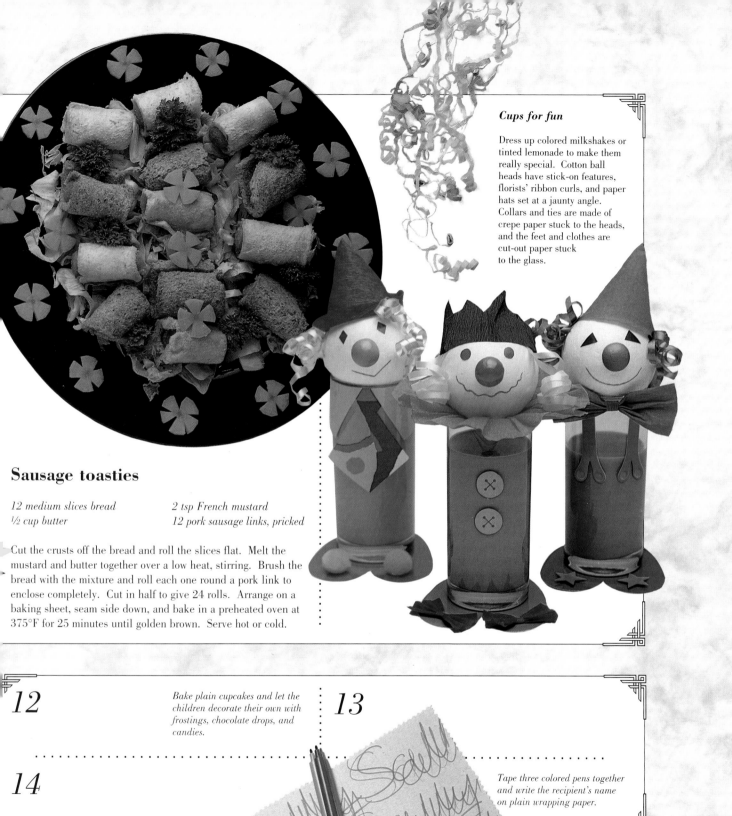

Dress up colored milkshakes or tinted lemonade to make them really special. Cotton ball heads have stick-on features, florists' ribbon curls, and paper hats set at a jaunty angle. Collars and ties are made of crepe paper stuck to the heads, and the feet and clothes are cut-out paper stuck to the glass.

Sausage toasties

12 medium slices bread
½ cup butter

2 tsp French mustard
12 pork sausage links, pricked

Cut the crusts off the bread and roll the slices flat. Melt the mustard and butter together over a low heat, stirring. Brush the bread with the mixture and roll each one round a pork link to enclose completely. Cut in half to give 24 rolls. Arrange on a baking sheet, seam side down, and bake in a preheated oven at 375°F for 25 minutes until golden brown. Serve hot or cold.

12

Bake plain cupcakes and let the children decorate their own with frostings, chocolate drops, and candies.

13

14

Tape three colored pens together and write the recipient's name on plain wrapping paper.

Christening parties

The centerpiece of many christening buffets is the cake, and combining cake and flowers can give stunning results. This simple white cake with its sophisticated and understated decoration is embellished with a wreath of white flowers—roses and moon daisies—with just a hint of blue added by the lavender, forget-me-nots, and chicory flower on the top.

A christening cake is usually a rich fruit cake—especially if the top tier of a wedding cake has been saved. But if you know your family likes a lighter cake, you can still use roll-out icing on a pound cake if you prefer.

To make a Godchild cocktail, pour lemonade over ice cubes in a tall glass and add a squeeze of lemon juice. Gently pour a measure of cassis liqueur on top, garnish with a lemon slice, and serve with straws.

15

16

A bowl of fresh fruit juice floating with real fruit slices and ice cubes makes a lovely party cup.

17

Small glasses of simple snowdrops make stunning table decorations for a winter party.

18

Chinese melon

12 ounces lean pork fillet, cubed
oil for brushing
salt and freshly ground black pepper
1 melon, chilled
1¾ cups canned pineapple pieces
2 tbsp olive oil
1 tbsp white wine vinegar
1 tsp soy sauce
1 clove garlic, crushed
pinch of ground ginger

Brush the pork with oil and season with salt and pepper. Thread on to skewers and broil until cooked, turning occasionally. Cool then chop. Halve the melon horizontally and remove the seeds. Remove the melon flesh and dice. Serrate the melon shells. Drain the pineapple and reserve the juice. Arrange the pork, melon, and pineapple in the melon shells. Mix 2 tbsp pineapple juice with the remaining ingredients and pour over the melon just before serving.

At a family event, make sure you select some foods which the children will enjoy.

Bible place cards

Cut 4½ x 3 in rectangles of white card and slightly smaller rectangles of paper. Glue them together down the center and fold lightly in half. Write the guest's name on the book pages and attach a piece of white ribbon to the top.

19

20

21

Scottish salmon trout

1 large salmon trout, boned
¼ cup butter
1 onion, finely minced
2 pounds spinach, steamed and chopped
¼ cup walnuts, chopped
1 cup dry bread crumbs
1 tbsp minced fresh parsley
1 tbsp minced fresh thyme
pinch of grated nutmeg
salt and freshly ground black pepper
juice of 2 lemons
1 lemon, sliced
1 bunch watercress

Lay the fish on a sheet of oiled foil. Heat a little butter and fry the onion until soft. Stir in the spinach, walnuts, bread crumbs, herbs, nutmeg, salt, pepper, and half the lemon juice. Stuff the fish and close the foil loosely over it. Bake in a preheated oven at 350°F for 35 minutes. Peel away the skin then transfer the fish to a serving platter. Dot with butter, sprinkle with lemon juice, and garnish with lemon and watercress.

Frozen oranges

A light dessert is often a good choice for a dinner party.

6 oranges
⅔ cup water
⅔ cup sugar
mint leaves

Slice the tops off the oranges and remove the pulp. Squeeze 1¼ cups juice. Whisk together the juice, water, and sugar. Pour into a freezer container and freeze until mushy. Whisk again, pour into the orange shells, and freeze. Serve garnished with mint.

22

23

Buy an attractive—and large—hostess apron to protect your clothes during last-minute preparations.

24

Tartan napkins will look very attractive with a plain white or matching colored cloth.

25

Stir one part whisky with one part sweet vermouth and three dashes of Benedictine to make a Bobby Burns cocktail.

A tartan wreath for Burns' Night

Wire three groups of red and white fresh or dried flowers into a twig ring. Make three bows from wide tartan ribbon and wire them into the ring between the flowers. Wire a ribbon tail behind one of the bows.

26

Burns' Night

27

28

Stick some tartan ribbon down the sides of simple white or colored place cards.

HILARY

MARK

A delightful table centerpiece

Early in the year, a vase of winter jasmine or a dried flower arrangement may be the simplest option for your table flowers and will look delightful, especially on a country-style table.

For a more sophisticated display, roses make a wonderful choice. Even if you do not have your own garden roses early in the year, you can always buy roses from the florist. If you have only a few roses, team them with simple greenery or a flower such as these umbellifer flowers to give depth and variety.

Simple and elegant napkins

Fold the napkin in half diagonally then bring the corners up to the apex. Turn the napkin over and fold up the bottom. Fold the sides underneath at a slight angle.

Don't forget to offer sliced lemon as well as cream at your tea party.

29

Serve several different teas: Earl Grey, herbal, and Chinese, for example.

30

31

Indoor bulbs make a lovely display for your table or a welcoming sight in the hall if you place them in an attractive basket.

Warming winter teas

There's perhaps nothing more welcoming than an old-fashioned tea laid out before a blazing fire. English muffins, soda bread, gingerbread, cream cake, and fruit cake—home-made or store-bought—give everyone an excellent choice. For a simple light fruit cake, rub 1 cup soft margarine into 3 cups self-rising flour then stir in ½ cup superfine sugar, 1½ cups mixed fruit, and 1 tsp mixed spice. Mix in 2 beaten eggs and enough milk to give a dropping consistency. Turn into a greased and lined 7-in cake pan, and bake in a preheated oven at 300°F for about 2 hours.

Guest list

February

ebruary is an excellent month for entertaining because the weather is so often inhospitable. It seems a long time since the pleasures of Christmas and a long time to wait for the joys of spring! Banish the cold with your own warmth and hospitality.

Duck in caper sauce

Choose unusual dishes for guests you want to impress.

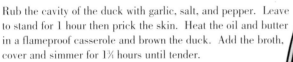

1 large duck
1 clove garlic, crushed
salt and freshly ground black pepper
1 tbsp oil
3 tbsp butter
1¼ cups chicken broth
4 tbsp sugar
⅔ cup water
1 tbsp white wine vinegar
6 tbsp capers
4 tsp cornstarch

Rub the cavity of the duck with garlic, salt, and pepper. Leave to stand for 1 hour then prick the skin. Heat the oil and butter in a flameproof casserole and brown the duck. Add the broth, cover and simmer for 1¾ hours until tender.

Meanwhile, gently dissolve the sugar in the water then boil to a caramel. Add the wine vinegar and 3 tablespoons of cooking liquid and bring to boiling, stirring. Transfer the duck to a warmed serving dish. Skim the stock, add the capers, and cornstarch mixed with water, and boil until the sauce clears. Add the caramel and stir until thick. Spoon a little sauce over the duck and serve the rest separately.

Equal parts of Cointreau, Tia Maria, and fresh cream shaken together make a Velvet Hammer cocktail to impress any guest.

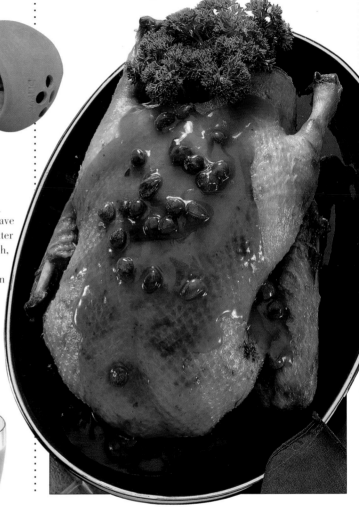

1

2

Select a menu allowing as much advance preparation as possible so you can spend your time with your guests.

3

4

Paper orchid

Fold a sheet of colored 8½ x 11 inch paper in quarters. Mark a ¼-in radius circle in the folded corner, mark the diagonal and midpoint lines, and cut to the circle on the lines and folds. Open out and number the corners. Tape together the corners with the same numbers, bringing the last four corners together underneath the bloom. Sit an orchid at each place setting.

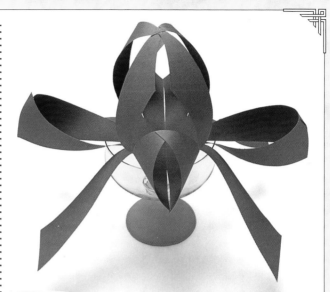

Chocolate artichoke

1 pound plain chocolate, grated
2½ tbsp oil
few drops of peppermint extract
1 globe artichoke
2 tbsp superfine sugar
2 tbsp butter
2½ tsp water
4 tbsp confectioners' sugar
3 tbsp cocoa powder
small round cake

Melt the chocolate and oil, stirring. Cool slightly then stir in the peppermint extract. Remove the artichoke leaves; dip the front of each leaf into the melted chocolate, lay on wax paper and leave overnight before peeling off.

Dissolve the sugar, butter, and water, then stir in the confectioners' sugar and cocoa. Cut the cake into a pyramid and cover with icing. Use more icing to stick the chocolate leaves on the cake.

5

6

Cut-glass decanters really show off the color of a good red wine and look wonderful on the table.

7

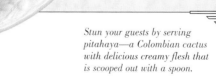

Stun your guests by serving pitahaya—a Colombian cactus with delicious creamy flesh that is scooped out with a spoon.

Hearts and flowers

For the sweet shortcrust:
⅓ cup butter
1¾ cups all-purpose flour
pinch of salt
1 tbsp sugar
3 tbsp water
1 egg, beaten

For the confectioners' custard:
1¼ cups milk
2 oz superfine sugar
2 tbsp cornstarch
3 egg yolks
few drops of vanilla extract
½ oz butter
4 cups raspberries

Rub the butter into the flour
and salt, then stir in the sugar. Mix in
the water to make a smooth dough
then leave to rest for 30 minutes.
Roll out and use to line a heart-shaped
pie pan. Glaze with egg. Bake blind in
a preheated oven at 400°F for 20
minutes. Cool.
    Bring the milk slowly to boiling.
Whisk the sugar, cornstarch, and egg yolks
until creamy. Add the vanilla extract
then stir in the milk. Return to a clean
saucepan and stir over a low heat until thick.
Beat in the butter then cool. Fill the tart with
the custard filling and top with the
raspberries. Garnish with fresh flowers.

8

9

10

11

*Cut a shape out of the top of a
gift box and glue in a round of
paper lace for a lovely effect.*

Straight from the heart

It is not difficult to find small, heart-shaped baskets or dishes to use as the base for your Valentine's Day table decoration, and the effect is worth that extra bit of effort. Cut dry foam to fit the container, and for a small arrangement choose delicate flowers in complementary colors, packing them together closely and working across the whole area of foam. Here, aquilegias, saxifrage, and pelargoniums combine with chives and anemones to give a delicate but lively effect.

Gift boxes

It is not difficult to buy heart-shaped gift boxes. You can glue on sequins or beads, or cover with attractive gift wrapping paper or fabric to make them special.

12

13

14

Valentine's Day

Forget the dozen red roses—a single beautiful bloom tied with a ribbon is far more romantic!

Round off your romantic dinner with a dessert wine such as Marsala or muscatel.

February

Chinese New Year feast

8 ounces vermicelli
4 shallots, sliced
5 tbsp oil
1 egg, beaten
2 cloves garlic, minced
2 tsp curry paste
½ cup shrimp
½ cup cooked chicken, sliced
½ cup chicken broth
½ cup beansprouts
2 tsp soy sauce
2 green onions (scallions), sliced
2 green chilies, sliced

Soak the vermicelli in warm water for 30 minutes then drain. Crisp-fry the shallots in a little oil. Drain. Make an omelet and cut into strips. Heat the remaining oil and fry the garlic until golden. Add the curry paste and fry for 1 minute. Add the shrimp, chicken, vermicelli, and broth and stir-fry until the liquid is almost absorbed. Add the beansprouts and soy sauce, and stir-fry for 2 minutes. Transfer to a warmed serving dish and garnish with the onions, omelet, green onions, and chilies.

Accompany with sesame-shrimp toasts. Mix 1 pound chopped shrimp, 1 egg white, 1 tbsp cornstarch, and a little salt and spread on rounds of bread. Garnish with strips of Canadian bacon and press sesame seeds into the top. Deep-fry until golden.

Select a jasmine or other Chinese tea from an oriental shop to serve with or after your feast.

Make noodle nests by deep-frying cooked noodles between two round draining spoons.

15

16

17

Write your guests' names on tiny Chinese lanterns made from thin colored paper as place cards and little gifts.

18

Make four or five cuts across a radish almost to the base, then cut again at right angles. Sprinkle with salt and leave for 30 minutes. Rinse and press into a lovely flower, adding greenery for the stalk and a carrot or red caviar center.

Hangchow fish

⅔ cup white wine
⅔ cup water
1 in ginger root,
    chopped
1 large bass
2 tbsp sugar
6 tbsp wine vinegar
2 tbsp soy sauce
1 tbsp cornstarch
1 clove garlic, crushed
1 carrot, thinly sliced
4 water chestnuts, thinly sliced
salt and freshly ground black pepper
4 green onions, diagonally sliced

Mix the wine, water, and half the ginger in a flameproof casserole. Slash the sides of the fish, add it to the casserole, cover and cook in a preheated oven at 350°F for 30 minutes. Transfer the fish to a warmed serving platter. Stir in the sugar, wine vinegar, soy sauce, and cornstarch and bring to boiling, stirring. Add the garlic, carrot, ginger, water chestnuts, and seasoning. Simmer, stirring, until thick, then pour over the fish and garnish with the green onions.

Lotus blossom napkins

Fold the four corners into the center of the napkin. Repeat this once more. Turn over the napkin and repeat again. Holding the center, pull the corners from behind the napkin so that they show beyond the corners of the square. Pull out the four single flaps.

Perfect posies

Many people like to give a little gift to their guests, and for an informal occasion it is easy to combine your table decoration with your parting gifts. Make some simple little posies by tying together a selection of dried flowers. Wrap a small band of paper lace around the outside and finish off with some curls of florists' ribbon to match the flower selection. The little basket will look lovely on the center of the table and your guests will be delighted to take home a memento of the occasion.

Pocket napkins

Quarter the napkin then fold in half to make a triangle. Fold down the top layer several times to make a band at the bottom, then fold over the top three corners as shown. Fold back the sides and decorate with a few fresh or dried flowers.

22

23

24

25

Wrap baked potatoes in aluminum foil and fill with chili, mushrooms in sauce, or grated cheeses.

Tomato and orange soup

Invite friends to enjoy a mug of hot soup with fresh crusty bread after a walk together on a crisp winter day.

¼ cup butter
1 onion, minced
3¼ cups pure tomato juice
juice and rind of 1 orange
1 tsp sugar
1 tbsp minced fresh parsley
salt and freshly ground black pepper
⅔ cup plain yogurt

Melt the butter and fry the onion until soft. Add the tomato juice, and orange juice and rind, bring to boiling and simmer for 5 minutes. Add the sugar and half the parsley, and season to taste. Purée until smooth or leave with a coarser texture. Stir in the yogurt and reheat gently before serving sprinkled with the remaining parsley.

26

27

*Don't just serve mulled wine
(see Dec 15) at Christmas—it is
perfect for any winter occasion.*

28

29

f you need an excuse for entertaining, March has plenty—from St David's Day to the first day of spring. If fresh flowers are too expensive during the winter, take advantage of the masses of daffodils and deck your rooms with a riot of spring blooms.

St David's Day lamb

2 tablespoons butter
1 onion, minced
¾ cup dried apricots, soaked and chopped
1 cup bread crumbs
2 oz flaked almonds
2 tbsp minced fresh parsley
juice of ½ lemon
salt and freshly ground black pepper
1–2 eggs, beaten
2 necks of lamb
2 tbsp all-purpose flour

Melt the butter and fry the onion until soft.
Mix with the apricots, bread crumbs, almonds,
parsley, and lemon juice and season with salt
and pepper. Mix in enough egg to bind.
Interlock the bones of the lamb and stuff the
central cavity. Dust lightly with flour and cook in
a preheated oven at 375°F for 30 minutes per 1 pound
plus 30 minutes. Transfer to a warmed serving platter
and leave to stand for 15 minutes before serving with fresh
spring vegetables.

A host of golden daffodils

Especially for those who are not confident about their skills
at flower-arranging, a simple vase of spring flowers makes
the perfect table centerpiece. Choose a wide container and
cut all the stems the same length. Arrange the flowers in the
container, making sure the stems all touch the bottom and the
flower heads are not too tightly bunched. Marbles are also
useful to hold the stems in place.

1

St David's Day

*Leeks are a must! Sauté them
lightly in oil with freshly snipped
chives and a little sesame oil.*

2

3

4

*Cut yellow card into a daffodil
shape and hand-write your
invitations in green ink.*

Paper daffodils

For each flower, enlarge and cut out six petals, one trumpet, one stamen, and two leaves from crepe paper. Wire the stamens round the top of a wire stem. Flute the trumpet edge, shape and wire it round the stamens. Wire the petals on the outside and the leaves to the stem, and bind with a strip of green crepe.

Soften strips of green leek tops in boiling water then drain well. Fold two strips of leek to form the sides of the bow and wrap a third piece round the center, trimming the ends.

5

6

7

Fold a long strip of paper in half lengthwise and snip along the folded edge then tape into small cutlet frills.

Planning a buffet

Choose a theme for your buffet meal. For a young lady's birthday party, this pink-themed spread offers a delicious range of foods. Don't offer too many dishes. If all your guests want to taste a little of everything, you will need more food than you anticipated.

A bowl of borscht, swirled with yogurt and sprinkled with chives, provides a tempting starter. Salmon mousse and shrimp cocktails are always popular, the latter spiced with tomato paste and dill. Glazed roast ham goes well with a salad featuring sharp-tasting radish and radicchio.

Dessert offers pink meringues, fondant cakes, strawberries marinated in orange juice and curaçao, and an ambrosial combination of whipped cream with plump yellow raisins, candied cherries, marshmallows, sliced bananas, and pineapple.

Line individual pastry cases with smoked salmon (lox) and top with a spoonful of scrambled egg sprinkled with chives.

Ginger ale cup

1 cup lump sugar
2 pts boiling water
½ cup lime juice
1 bottle ginger ale, chilled
½ orange, sliced
mint sprigs

Dissolve the sugar in the water then cool and chill. Mix the syrup with the lime juice and ginger ale in a punch bowl or large jug, add some ice cubes and garnish with fruit and mint.

8

Arrange the buffet table so that guests serve themselves main items first, followed by side-dishes then desserts.

9

10

11

If you have a large number of guests, arrange for someone to help to serve the buffet; as hostess you will be far too busy.

Cutlery envelope napkins

Fold the napkin in quarters. Fold the top layer of fabric down diagonally two or three times to make a band across the center. Make thinner folds in the next layer and tuck it under the first fold. Fold back the sides.

12

13

14

Beat 10 chopped anchovy fillets with a little butter and lemon juice, then spread on toast

squares. Broil until bubbling then top with sliced, stuffed olives.

Irish beef

Guinness (or other dark beer) tastes wonderful served with a rich beef casserole.

2 tbsp oil
1½ lb chuck steak, cubed
2 onions, sliced
2 tbsp all-purpose flour
1 clove garlic, crushed
1¼ cups Guinness
1¼ cups water
1 bouquet garni
pinch of sugar
dash of red wine vinegar
salt and freshly ground black pepper
American mustard
6 thick slices French bread

Heat the oil in a Dutch oven and brown the meat on all sides then remove. Add the onions and sauté until soft, then stir in the flour, garlic, Guinness, water, and seasonings. Bring to boiling, stirring, then return the meat to the pan, cover, and cook in a preheated oven at 325°F for 2½ hours, skimming any fat from the surface 15 minutes before the end of cooking time. Spread the mustard on the bread and spoon a little of the fat over it. Arrange the bread on to the top of the casserole and cook, uncovered, for 20 minutes until the bread is crisp.

Mix 3 dashes of green chartreuse and 3 dashes of crème de menthe with 3 tbsp of vermouth and 3 tbsp of Irish whiskey to make a stunning Shamrock cocktail.

Potpourri gifts

Potpourri makes an inexpensive and attractive gift. Fill little boxes with fragrant potpourri and glue a strip of matching ribbon to the bottom of the box so that you can tie it in a pretty bow on the top.

15

16

17

St Patrick's Day

18

Lace strong, sweetened black coffee with Irish whiskey then float whipped cream on top.

Herb posies

Tie together a collection of fresh herbs with satin ribbon to arrange at each place setting as decorative gifts. Select herbs with different leaf shapes and textures, and include a few herbs in flower to add the subtle contrast of the petal colors.

Make your place cards out of green card folded in half then cut into a shamrock shape.

19

20   First day of spring   21

ELIZABETH

The welcome of spring

Nothing is quite as welcoming to a guest as a vase of lovely flowers, and in spring there are plenty to choose from, all with wonderful, vibrant colors and including many— such as philadelphus and hyacinths—with beautiful fragrances.

Arrangements do not have to be elaborate, and you can use the simplest of containers for your display. If you have chosen a loosely-structured and lively collection of flowers to brighten the entrance, for example, a sophisticated vase would be quite out of place.

22

Garnish slices of smoked salmon and a little chicory on buttered rye bread with a lemon twist and dill sprig.

23

24

25

Scoop ice cream, nuts, fruit, and sauce into tall glasses for a simple but attractive dessert.

Colorful fruits or vegetables make unusual table decorations, especially if scattered with a few bright flower heads.

Country fruit wines

There are many country wines now available made from fruits such as apricots, strawberries, elderberries, or blueberries—or you might make your own. They are not necessarily as sweet as you might expect, and make a pleasant change from your usual wines to serve at a spring luncheon party—as well as providing a conversation piece for your guests.

26

27

28

For a light starter, wrap slices of melon in raw smoked ham and garnish with parsley.

Chicken with lime

4 chicken halves
salt and freshly ground black pepper
1 tsp chopped fresh basil
6 tbsp olive oil

4 limes
1 tsp sugar
2 basil sprigs

Trim and flatten the chicken, and remove the backbone. Season and sprinkle with basil. Place in a shallow bowl and pour 2 tbsp oil and the juice of 2 limes over it. Cover and marinate in the refrigerator for 4 hours. Remove from the marinade, brush with a little oil, and broil until browned on both sides. Place in a roasting pan, sprinkle with the remaining oil, and roast in a preheated oven at 375°F for 30 minutes. Peel and thinly slice the remaining limes and arrange on top of the chicken. Sprinkle with sugar and broil for a few minutes until the sugar caramelizes. Place on a warmed serving platter, and spoon over any remaining marinade and the cooking juices. Serve garnished with basil.

Special occasion posies

Make your special occasion gift posies a little different by arranging a collection of tiny spring flowers such as grape hyacinths, primroses, wallflowers, sweet violets, and white pulmonaria. Wrap paper lace round the posy and secure at the back to create a pretty collar to complete the gift and tie a few curled florists' ribbons to the flower stems.

29

Sift confectioners' sugar through paper lace to decorate the top of a plain cake.

30

31

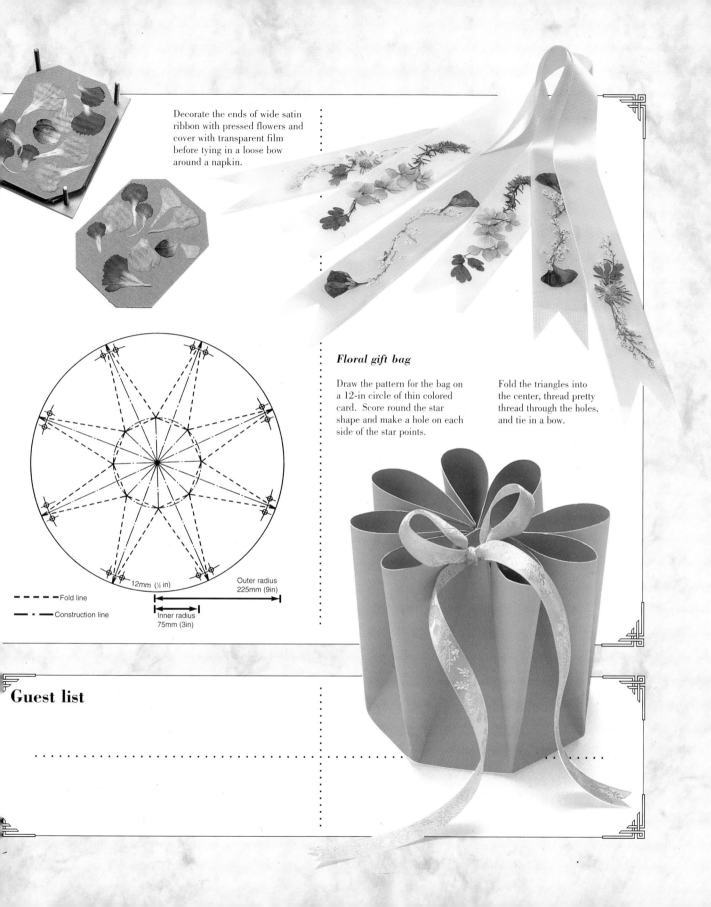

Decorate the ends of wide satin ribbon with pressed flowers and cover with transparent film before tying in a loose bow around a napkin.

Floral gift bag

Draw the pattern for the bag on a 12-in circle of thin colored card. Score round the star shape and make a hole on each side of the star points.

Fold the triangles into the center, thread pretty thread through the holes, and tie in a bow.

- - - - - Fold line

— · — · — Construction line

12mm (½ in)

Inner radius
75mm (3in)

Outer radius
225mm (9in)

Guest list

· ·

April

*A*pril is a mixed month for entertaining in some

parts. Just when the blossoms are at their most beautiful

and you begin to think you can move outside, along come

those showers and blustery breezes to send you back into

the warmth of the house.

Easter simnel cake

1 cup butter
grated rind and juice of 2 lemons
¾ cup mixed candied peel
1 cup superfine sugar
4 eggs
¾ cup seedless yellow
*   raisins*
2¼ cups currants
3½ cups all-purpose flour
pinch of salt
1 tsp baking powder
1 tsp pumpkin pie spice
12 ounces marzipan
2 tbsp apricot jam, sieved

Cream the butter, lemon rind, and sugar until light. Gradually beat in the eggs then stir in the peel and fruits. Fold in the dry ingredients. Spoon half the mixture into a greased and lined 8-in cake pan. Roll out one-third of the marzipan to a 8-in circle, lay it in the pan, and fill with the remaining mixture. Bake in a preheated oven at 325°F for 1 hour then reduce to 300°F for a further 2½ hours. Roll out half the remaining marzipan into a circle. Brush the cake with jam and place the marzipan on top. Roll the remaining marzipan into 11 balls and arrange round the cake. Brush with beaten egg white and brown under a broiler. Decorate with chocolate eggs and flowers.

1

As an Easter table centerpiece, hang colorful Easter eggs and decorations on an arrangement of twigs.

2

3

4

Buy a butter curler so you can serve a bowl of pretty butter twists.

Decoupage eggs

Cover hard-cooked eggs, one side at a time, with a layer of household glue. Cover with another layer of glue and stick on tiny cut-out paper shapes or decorations. When dry, cover with a final layer of glue.

Cover a plain cake with butter frosting and decorate with chocolate sticks, chocolate sprinkles, and sugar-coated chocolate eggs for every child's favorite Easter cake.

5

6

Add food coloring to the boiling water, then decorate your breakfast eggs with felt pen faces or patterns.

7

Entertaining on an outing

Taking the kids and a few special friends on an Easter holiday outing need not mean just sandwiches and potato chips. Be adventurous and take sausage rolls, pizza slices, savory pastries, or homemade Scotch eggs.

4 hard-cooked eggs
2 cups sausagemeat
1 egg, beaten
4 tbsp bread crumbs
1 tsp mixed herbs
1 tbsp all-purpose flour
oil for deep-frying

Coat the eggs with sausagemeat and brush with beaten egg. Mix the bread crumbs and herbs then roll the eggs in the mixture. Deep-fry in moderately hot oil for 10 minutes. Drain well.

8

9

Ice rectangular cookies like dominoes for a simple and fun serving idea.

10

Take plenty of drinks on a kids' outing or make sure you can buy more if necessary.

11

Portable candy dish

Using a square of colored paper, fold the corners to the center. Turn it over and repeat then fold the corners from the center to the outside edges. Turn over and fold the center points to the corners. Gently squeeze the corners to open up the dish to fill with candies or nuts and raisins.

Ask your guests to bring a small backsack and pack up the lunches individually so they can carry their own.

Rolls with a difference

To keep the children busy, they can help you to bake some rolls for their outing—almost foolproof if you use active dry yeast and make sure that they are well kneaded. For interesting fillings, try sliced tomato and tunafish, salami and mushrooms, cottage cheese and walnuts, banana and honey, salmon and radicchio. Use interesting breads such as pumpernickel, pastrami on rye bread, or prosciutto on ciabatta.

12

13

14

The journey home from an outing can be boring—have some amusing travel games or songs in reserve.

Princess napkins

Fold each half of the napkin in toward the center line and back on itself then fold the napkin in half to make a concertina. Fold the edges in toward the center and back on themselves. Pull one corner across toward the opposite corner, making a triangle, then repeat with the remaining folds. Ease the folds open slightly to display.

15	*Extra-virgin olive oil with its distinctive flavor is the best to use for salad dressings.*	16	
17		18	*Once you have tasted freshly-grated Parmesan, you will never again buy it ready-grated.*

Italian-style grouper

1 pound mushrooms
1 clove garlic, chopped
3 tbsp olive oil
juice of 1 lemon
1 tbsp chopped fresh parsley
2 tsp chopped fresh basil
1 tsp chopped fresh sage
4 tbsp dry white wine
½ tsp cornstarch
few drops of anchovy extract
4 red grouper, cleaned
1 tbsp bread crumbs
1 tbsp freshly grated Parmesan cheese
2 sprigs basil

Fry the mushrooms and garlic in the oil until slightly softened.
Add the lemon juice, herbs, wine, and cornstarch, and simmer
until thickened. Stir in the anchovy extract. Place the fish
close together in a shallow ovenproof dish. Pour in the sauce
and sprinkle with bread crumbs and Parmesan. Cover loosely
with foil and cook in a preheated oven at 375°F for 20 minutes.
Remove the foil and cook for a further 10 minutes to brown the
fish. Serve garnished with basil.

The Italians love oysters simply
sprinkled with parsley, garlic,
and bread crumbs, drizzled with
olive oil, and baked for 10
minutes in a hot oven.

Capucine mocktail

Serve this delicious mocktail to all
your guests—whatever their
age. Shake together one part
peppermint cordial with four
parts fresh cream. Strain and
add crushed ice. Finely grate a
little plain chocolate over the top.

*Italian wines
are robust and
well flavored—
perfect for serving
with rich dishes.*

19

20

21

Traditional Sunday lunch

Entertain your friends to the best of British cooking: roast beef, roast potatoes, and Yorkshire pudding with lightly steamed fresh vegetables. Always slow-roast beef for the best flavor and choose a joint with a little fat—such as London broil—as it will stay moister during cooking. The meat should be slightly pink and succulent in the center when ready. Parboil potatoes before roasting them in the pan with the meat so that they absorb the wonderful flavors, then make your gravy with the skimmed meat juices while the roast rests before carving.

The perfect Yorkshire pudding mix is ⅔ cup milk, 1 egg, ½ cup all-purpose flour, and a pinch of salt, poured into hot fat in hot pans and cooked at 400°F for about 20 minutes.

To make a tomato rose garnish, start at the base and cut a thin spiral of tomato skin. Lay the skin flesh side down and roll up, using a cocktail stick to spread the petals gently.

22	23	St George's Day
		Wear a red rose in your buttonhole to celebrate a traditionally English day!
24		25
	Serve a selection of mustards and horseradish sauce to complement the roast beef.	

A circle of roses

Fix a circle of dry foam to a pin
holder in the center of a deep
plate. Fix a rose in the center
and surround with blue flowers.
Arrange a circle of lobelia and
an outer ring of roses.

To finish the meal

Fancy chocolates or dessert mints can be arranged in scallop
shells to make an unusual and attractive end to a meal. Fold
a red napkin in half to make a triangle and lay it on a dessert
plate. Top with a small round of paper lace then a scallop
shell filled with chocolates. Tie a length of red ribbon into
a bow with long tails and attach to the base of the shell.

26

27

*Contrast a pure white linen cloth
with startling red napkins.*

28

April

A vegetarian feast

1 tbsp oil
1 onion, minced
4 tomatoes, skinned and sliced
1 cup cooked black-eyed peas
⅔ cup broth
1¼ cups sweet cider
1 tsp sugar
2 carrots, chopped
2 small turnips, sliced
2 sticks celery, chopped
2 heads broccoli, cut into flowerets
¼ cauliflower, cut into flowerets
1 tbsp all-purpose flour
2 tbsp chopped fresh parsley
salt and freshly ground black pepper
3 oz butter
4 oz whole-wheat flour
2 oz rolled oats
4 oz Cheddar cheese, grated

Heat the oil and sauté the onion until soft. Place in a greased
ovenproof dish with the tomatoes and beans. Bring the broth,
cider, sugar, carrots, and turnips to boiling and simmer until
tender. Place the vegetables in the dish. Add the celery,
broccoli, and cauliflower to the pan and simmer until tender.
Place with the other vegetables. Mix the flour and parsley
into the pan and cook, stirring, until thickened. Simmer for
2 minutes then pour over the vegetables and season.
    Rub the butter into the flour then stir in the oats, cheese,
and seasoning. Sprinkle this over the vegetables and press down
lightly. Bake in a preheated oven
at 400°F for 35 minutes until
golden brown.

29

30

*Don't assume vegetarian guests
will eat fish; always ask before
you plan your menu.*

An unusual
presentation can make
all the difference when
you are entertaining.
This crunchy
salad looks
splendid in its
red cabbage cup.

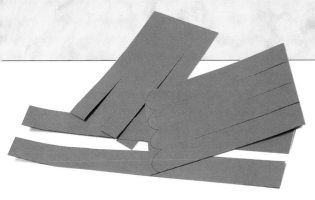

Paper baskets

Cut two 4 x 12 in sheets of
contrasting colored paper, fold
in half, and scallop the short
edges. Cut into 1-in
strips, stopping 1 in away
from the open end. Weave
the strips together by placing
one strip alternately between
the layers of the other. Cut a
strip for a handle and glue it
inside the basket.

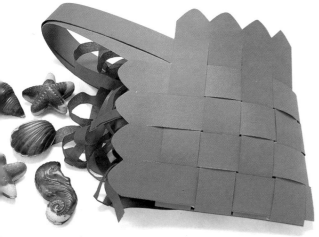

Peach Melba dessert

1¼ cups water
¾ cup sugar
juice of ½ lemon
1 tbsp kirsch
4 cups raspberries
6 peaches, peeled and pitted
2½ cups vanilla ice cream

Bring the water, sugar,
lemon juice, kirsch, and
raspberries to the boil,
boil for 5 minutes then cool
and purée. Chill. Arrange
the peaches in individual
glasses and add scoops of
ice cream. Pour a little
sauce over them and garnish
with mint sprigs.

Guest list

May

With the coming of May, spring really has arrived and it is often a busy time for entertaining as people shake off the cobwebs of winter. Make the most of the abundant spring flowers to make a welcoming decoration for your guests.

May Day chicken salad

2 tbsp butter
3 chicken breasts
⅔ cup dry white wine
¾ cup chicken broth
5 tbsp heavy cream
salt and freshly ground black pepper
4 tomatoes, skinned
2 avocados, peeled, pitted, and sliced
juice of 1 lemon
5 cups mixed green salad, shredded

Melt the butter and quickly seal the chicken on all sides. Stir in the wine and broth, and simmer until reduced by half. Cover and simmer gently until the chicken is tender. Remove and slice the chicken. Stir in the cream and season. Simmer, stirring, until the sauce thickens. Thinly slice 2 tomatoes and dice the others. Sprinkle the avocados with lemon juice as soon as they have been prepared. Arrange the lettuce on a serving platter, and alternate the avocado and tomato slices around the edge. Top with the chicken, sprinkle with diced tomato, and spoon the sauce over it.

Oriental fan napkins

Fold a well-starched napkin in half lengthwise then fold into concertina folds to just past the center. Fold in half lengthwise then fold the loose end of the napkin across on the diagonal. Fold the flap underneath to support the napkin and fan out the folds.

1	May Day	2	*A lace cloth over a plain contrasting tablecloth gives an attractive and unusual effect.*
3		4	

Cut a bulbous green onion in half in a Van Dyck pattern. Stand in iced water tinted with a few drops of food coloring to make beautiful onion waterlilies to garnish salads.

Wrap ribbons around a pencil and twist them from the top to pin at the edges of a cake like a maypole.

5

6

7

In the springtime, wines are a perfect accompaniment to seasonal celebrations.

Spanish paella

12 mussels, scrubbed and bearded
6 clams, scrubbed
3 chorizo sausages
2 tbsp olive oil
8 cups diced chicken
1 onion, chopped
2 cloves garlic, crushed
2 bell peppers, shredded
2 cups long-grain rice
pinch of saffron
5 cups boiling water
salt and freshly ground black pepper
12 large peeled shrimp
¾ cup diced cod or red snapper
½ cup frozen peas
3 tomatoes, skinned and chopped

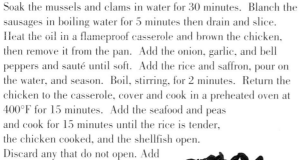

Soak the mussels and clams in water for 30 minutes. Blanch the
sausages in boiling water for 5 minutes then drain and slice.
Heat the oil in a flameproof casserole and brown the chicken,
then remove it from the pan. Add the onion, garlic, and bell
peppers and sauté until soft. Add the rice and saffron, pour on
the water, and season. Boil, stirring, for 2 minutes. Return the
chicken to the casserole, cover and cook in a preheated oven at
400°F for 15 minutes. Add the seafood and peas
and cook for 15 minutes until the rice is tender,
the chicken cooked, and the shellfish open.
Discard any that do not open. Add
the tomatoes, heat through for
5 minutes then serve.

8

*Fold a black-painted paper lace
round in sixteenths from the
center, slit along one fold, concertina the folds, stick to a strip
of card and add a paper rose.*

9

10

11

*Try imported Spanish wines to
accompany your paella, or serve
a rich California zinfandel.*

Avocado, orange, and olive salad

Presentation makes all the difference when you are entertaining guests. This beautiful salad looks stunning but is quite simple to make. Simply slice 2 avocados, 2 oranges, and some olives and sprinkle with basil and some sliced red onion. Make a dressing of 1 tbsp of white wine vinegar, 4 tbsp of olive oil, ½ tsp of mustard, and salt and pepper to pour over the salad when you are ready to serve.

Make Sangria to serve with your Spanish feast. Slice 1 lime, 1 lemon, and 1 orange. Mix with 5 tbsp sugar, 4 tbsp brandy, and a bottle of red wine. Chill well, then add 2½ cups chilled club soda or mineral water just before serving.

Spanish luminarios

Make these party lights for indoor or outdoor entertaining, but position them carefully for safety. Use small, flat-based paper bags and turn over the top to make a cuff. Fold the bag lengthwise into quarters and cut or punch out shapes along the edges. Fill the bag with a little sand and stand a nightlight in the bottom.

Bottled sweet mini-peppers can be stuffed with cream cheese as a tasty cocktail snack.

A fishy dish

If you don't have the right platter in which to serve your seafood, make one! Roll out 1 lb of puff pastry dough and cut a fish shape, and a few small fish from the trimmings. Score round the fish ½ in from the edge. Mark scales and an eye, brush with beaten egg and bake in a preheated oven at 400°F for 10 minutes. Lift out the center lid. Make a white sauce and stir in 4 cups of chunks of cooked, mixed white fish such as red snapper, cod, smoked whitefish, and shrimp, flavored with tarragon. Fill the fish, cover with the lid, and reheat in the oven before serving garnished with tarragon.

15

Serve chocolate-covered coffee beans from good candy stores as a sophisticated end to your dinner.

16

17

18

If you entertain frequently, invest in two coffee pots so you never have to wait for more coffee.

Pressed flower candles

Candles always make lovely table centers, combining subtle light and beauty. Transform ordinary thick candles by sticking on pressed flowers or leaves round the base and covering the designs with transparent adhesive film. Do not let the candle burn down to the decoration.

A pretty mixture of garden flowers—honeysuckle, lily-of-the-valley, thrift, anemones, and geraniums—casually arranged in a glass makes a lovely room decoration or table centerpiece for an informal dinner.

19

20

21

Look out for unusual cheeses from small dairies, instead of using mass-produced cheeses on your cheeseboard.

Treats for teenagers

Don't go overboard with complicated dishes for a teenage party—
opt for a delicious and simple dish such as the ever-popular pizza.

1 package active dry yeast
2 cups all-purpose flour
pinch of salt
1 tsp sugar
3 tbsp olive oil
1 cup warm water
1 onion, minced
1 clove garlic, crushed
2 cups pure tomato juice
1 tbsp tomato paste
1 tsp oregano
salt and freshly ground black pepper
½ cup shredded mozzarella cheese
4 tbsp black olives, pitted
2 tbsp anchovies, drained
½ each red and green bell pepper, sliced
2 tbsp freshly grated Parmesan cheese

Mix the yeast with the sugar and half the water. Cover and let
foam for 20 minutes. Mix the flour, salt, and 2 tbsp olive oil.
Add the yeast mixture and the rest of the water, and mix to a
dough, kneading until smooth and elastic. Cover and leave to
rise until doubled in size. Meanwhile, heat the remaining oil
and sauté the onion and garlic until soft. Add the tomato juice
and paste, oregano, and seasoning. Simmer, stirring, until thick.
Press the dough into a circle on a greased cookie sheet. Cover
with tomato sauce, sprinkle with half the mozzarella, arrange the
topping ingredients then finish with the mozzarella and
Parmesan. Bake in a preheated oven at 400°F for 20 minutes.

PAULA

BEN TOM

22	23
24	25

Cut original gift tags or place cards in the shape of the recipient's name in overlapping letters.

EMMA

Healthy nibbles

Teenagers love to nibble, so make a selection of dips and serve them with strips of fresh vegetables. Here are a few ideas: mayonnaise flavored with mango chutney, curry paste, cream, and cumin; puréed avocados and onion with lemon juice and garlic; softened onion cooked with tomatoes, mixed with grated cheese, bread crumbs, and egg then puréed with mustard and thick, natural yogurt.

Pour equal parts of orange juice and ginger ale over ice cubes in a tall glass. Garnish with a sliced orange and a cherry, and serve this Nursery Fizz with straws.

26

27

28

Banned from a teenage party? Take a casserole and some wine to enjoy with the neighbors.

Caribbean fruit salad

3 peaches
3 kiwi fruits
1 star fruit (carambola)
½ cup strawberries, halved
⅔ cup blueberries
2 mangoes, peeled and chopped
juice of ½ lime
a few strawberry leaves

Blanch the peaches in boiling water for a few
seconds then peel, halve, pit, and slice. Peel
and slice the kiwi fruits, trim and slice the
star fruit. Arrange the prepared fruits and
the strawberries in an attractive pattern on
a large platter and sprinkle with half the
blueberries. Purée the mango flesh with
half the lime juice and the remaining
blueberries, then rub through a sieve.
Pour this over the fruits, garnish with
strawberry leaves, and chill.

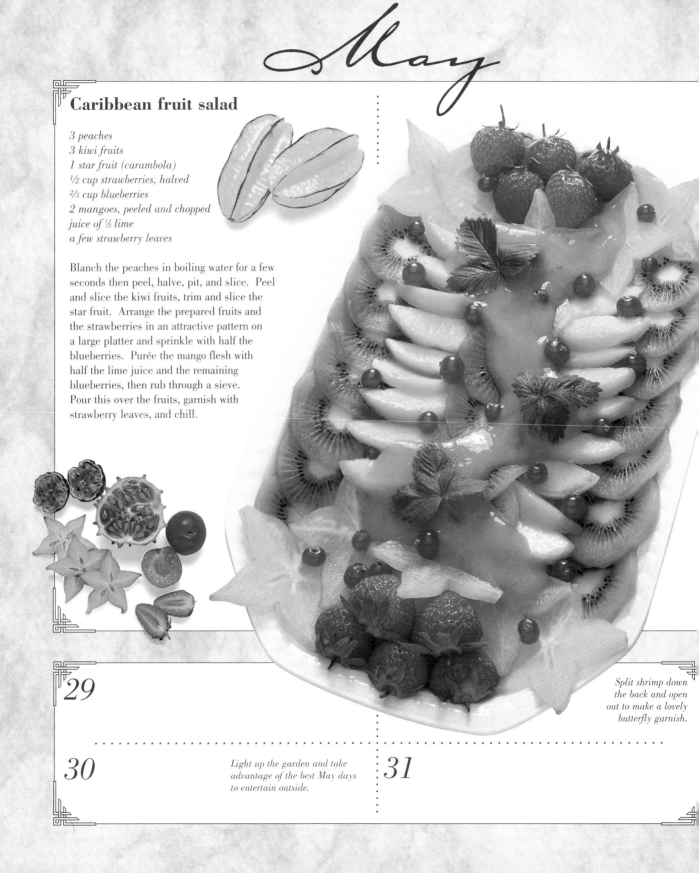

*Split shrimp down
the back and open
out to make a lovely
butterfly garnish.*

29

30   *Light up the garden and take
advantage of the best May days
to entertain outside.*

31

Rum Fix cocktail

A rum-based cocktail is a must for Caribbean-style entertaining. Stir 1 tsp of sugar syrup or light corn syrup with the juice of ½ a lemon, 3 tbsp of rum, and 3 tbsp of cherry brandy. Pour over crushed ice in a tall glass and garnish with fruit.

Hot rum coffee

Place 6 lumps of sugar, the rind of 2 oranges, 6 cloves, and a cinnamon stick in a saucepan and cover the sugar with rum. Stir over a low heat until the sugar has dissolved and the mixture is almost boiling. Strain into cups of hot black coffee.

Paper fruit bowl

Paper decorations can often be pressed into service to create an unusual table centerpiece. This bowl of paper fruit creates just the right style for a lively Caribbean spread.

Guest list

here are endless ways to be original in your

entertaining, and when there is such a range of foods in

the stores and so many flowers in the garden it is often

difficult to choose. Make a rule to be selective. Quality is

more stylish than quantity.

Afternoon tea in the garden

Afternoon tea in the garden is a lovely way to entertain friends and family when the weather is fine and the garden is at its best. Simple white linen is the ideal choice, graced with pretty tableware. Keep the foods simple but beautifully prepared and presented: tiny sandwiches of cucumber or salmon, delicate cookies or pastries. Echo the flowers in your table decoration by arranging some flower heads round your cake or garnishing food with a single bloom. Sweet peas, cornflowers, and daisies transform the effect of this frosted sponge cake and make it look twice as delicious.

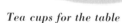

Tea cups for the table

A selection of pretty tea cups make lovely containers for flower decorations to scatter over your table. Fill the cups with water and cut the flower stems to the right length. Arrange a few flower heads and a little greenery in each tea cup.

1

2

Always have a contingency plan for outdoor entertaining in case the weather lets you down.

3

Use a hostess cart to take everything you need outside before your guests arrive.

4

Dressed Dungeness crab

Dressed Dungeness crab makes a lovely centerpiece for a garden high tea. Pull off the crab claws and pull the body from the main shell. Remove and discard the stomach bag and the gray feathered gills. Take out all the meat, separating dark and light. Crack the top of the shell and remove the pieces. Scrub and dry the shell then brush it with oil. Remove the meat from the claws. Arrange strips of dark and light meats alternately in the shell, garnish with chopped fresh parsley and arrange on a bed of lettuce. Serve with salad and brown bread.

Apple slices, chopped celery, and walnuts dressed with 3 tbsp olive oil, 1 tbsp wine vinegar, a pinch of mustard, salt and pepper makes a delicious salad to serve with cold meats.

June

Birthday breakfast cake

For those with a sense of fun, make a fruity cake in a pan the same size as your skillet. Use white roll-out frosting and apricot halves to make fried eggs. Color the frosting before molding into sausage links, and brush the frosting lightly with sieved apricot jam to give a shine. You'll have them reaching for the tomato sauce!

If you doubt your abilities at cake decorating, color roll-out icing and knead it unevenly for a marbled effect. Cover the cake and trim the edges. Cut a strip of paper to fit round the sides and fold it like a concertina. Cut out an animal design through all the layers, making sure they are joined at the edges. Tape round the cake and add the candles.

Licorice candies provide endless possibilities for decorating children's cakes.

8

9

10

11

Make cakes in candy paper cases for a children's party and decorate with M&Ms.

Children's party cakes

The effect is all-important when making children's cakes—not the accuracy or level of difficulty. Aim for a simple design and make use of ready-made roll-out frosting, buttercream frosting, shaped cake pans, or stencils to make the job easier. This lovely spider's web cake is a chocolate sponge. Sift 1½ cups confectioners' sugar and mix in just enough water to make a coating consistency. Spread over the top of the cake then immediately pipe circles of melted chocolate and draw a knife through the circles to make the web pattern. Cover the sides with buttercream frosting and chocolate sprinkles. The spiders are made with chocolate marshmallows, chocolate buttons, and licorice, pressed together with a little buttercream frosting.

Cut large and small rectangles of chocolate cake, sandwich one on top of the other with buttercream frosting and cover with more frosting. Press chocolate buttons down the sides and make the treads and gun barrel with chocolate flake.

12

Brush the underside of washed rose leaves with melted chocolate then peel them away when set.

13

14

Zigeunerschnitzel

If you choose to entertain your guests German-style, you should work out how to pronounce the name of this delicious veal dish—if you can't, call it gypsy scallops.

8 veal scallops
3 tbsp all-purpose flour
salt and freshly ground black pepper
3 tbsp butter
1 onion, thinly sliced
1 red bell pepper, thinly sliced
1 green bell pepper, thinly sliced
1 tbsp paprika
1 cup beef broth
⅔ cup plain yogurt, beaten

Dredge the scallops in a little flour and seasoning. Heat the butter until foaming and brown the scallops. Remove from the skillet. Add the onion and bell peppers and fry for 3 minutes. Remove from the pan. Stir in the flour and cook, stirring, until golden brown. Add the paprika and cook for 1 minute. Whisk in the broth and bring to boiling. Return the veal and bell peppers to the pan, cover, and cook for 10 minutes until the veal is tender. Transfer to a warmed serving plate and drizzle over the yogurt.

Arrange halved seedless grapes in dessert glasses and sprinkle with crème de menthe. Top with sour cream, sprinkle with brown sugar and garnish with mint sprigs.

Bishop's hat napkins

Fold the napkin in half diagonally then fold the corners to the top to make a square. Turn the napkin over and fold in half diagonally to make a triangle. Pull into a circle and tuck one end into the other to secure. Pull down the side flaps.

15

16

With a corer in the base of a large radish, cut away the outside of the base and circles from the cap to make a red-capped mushroom.

17

Serve German wines or light Californian wines to go with German food.

18

Sauerkraut salad

2 carrots, grated
1 red apple, diced
1 onion, chopped
juice of 1 lemon
1 large can sauerkraut,
*   soaked and drained*
5 tbsp olive oil
2 tbsp white wine vinegar
1 tsp sugar
1 tsp cinnamon
salt and freshly ground
*   black pepper*

Mix the carrots, apple, onion, and lemon juice in a bowl then add the sauerkraut. Mix the remaining ingredients, pour over the salad, and toss together thoroughly.

19

20

21

First day of summer

For an informal meal, many guests will enjoy chilled imported German or Czech beer.

Summer buffet selection

Mix ⅔ cup plain yogurt, 2 chopped red peppers, 1 tsp chopped mint, 1 cup shrimp, fill hollowed-out chunks of cucumber and sprinkle with paprika. Wrap wedges of ripe melon with slices of raw smoked ham.

Blend 1 cup canned sardines, ¾ cup cream cheese, 6 tbsp soured cream, 1 tsp chopped onion, 1 tsp mild mustard, ½ tsp paprika. Slice the tops off 4 lemons, remove the pulp, and mix half the juice into the sardines. Refill the lemons, garnish with olives, and serve with toast.

Purée 8 ounces smoked trout with the juice of 1 lemon, 1 tbsp sherry, and a few drops of tabasco sauce. Fold in ¼ pt whipped cream and fill rolls of smoked salmon.

Halve 4 hard-cooked eggs and blend the yolks with 5 anchovy fillets, ¼ cup shrimp, ¼ cup butter, 2 tbsp whipping cream. Spoon into the egg whites and garnish the chives and olives.

Summer fruit cup

It looks lovely and it tastes wonderful—the perfect fruit cup for a midsummer ball.

2 bottles light white wine
2 bottles sparkling wine
¼ of a fifth of gin
sliced strawberries
sliced mandarins

Mix all the liquids together and sweeten to taste with a little sugar syrup, if you like. Pour over ice cubes in a punch bowl and add the sliced fruits to taste. Serve with a little fruit floating in the glasses.

Masks for your midsummer ball

Cut a mask shape from thin card, cover with florescent or satin fabric, and clip and glue back the edges. Stick on tiny beads, sequins, feathers, shapes cut from gold paper lace or curls of florists' ribbon. Decorate and stick on a piece of cane or kabob skewer for the stick.

22

23

24

25

Music helps to set atmosphere so make a careful selection to suit the occasion.

26

27

Set up your outdoor Christmas lights in the garden or use barbecue flares.

28

Loop swathes of ivy or other greenery around the table and punctuate with little posies of flowers with trailing ribbons.

Beef casserole

Welcome guests home after a theater trip with a warming casserole served with French bread, salad, and a glass of red wine.

2 lb beef, cubed
1 tbsp all-purpose flour
2 tbsp oil
5 cups boiling water
1 cup mixed fruit juice
1 lb small potatoes
1 cup carrots, sliced
2 cups turnips, cubed
1 cup pearl onions
½ cup red wine
salt and freshly ground black pepper

Coat the beef in flour. Heat the oil in a flameproof casserole and brown the beef. Add all the remaining ingredients, bring to boiling, then cover and cook in a preheated oven at 325°F for about 2 hours. Thicken the gravy, if necessary, by stirring in a spoonful of cornstarch blended with a little water and simmer for 2 minutes. Check and adjust the seasoning to taste.

A few perfect blooms floating in a shallow bowl take seconds to put together yet add a luxurious and special touch to a table. A few lemon geranium leaves add a touch of fragrance.

29

If you prefer a cold collation, serve a selection of cold meats with unusual salads.

Guest list

30

Carrot and celery salad

A crunchy salad goes well with a rich beef casserole and can be left in the refrigerator ready for your guests.

1 cup carrots, diced
½ cup celery, sliced
1 red bell pepper, diced
⅔ cup walnuts, chopped
4 tbsp corn kernels
1 tsp paprika
pinch of chili powder
4 tbsp French dressing

Mix all the ingredients together well and chill for 30 minutes before serving.

For a late supper, choose foods which can be prepared, covered, and left ready for your return.

Four feathers napkins

Fold a napkin in half diagonally. Placing your finger on the center of the folded edge and, using the top layer, bring the apex of the triangle across to the left-hand corner. Repeat twice. Turn the napkin over and roll into a loose cone. Fold up the bottom, arrange the napkin in a glass, and straighten the folds.

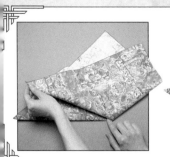

*J*uly is the height of summer and packed with
opportunities to entertain your friends before the vacation
season. Pick this month for a summer buffet, a formal
dinner party, or casual drinks with close friends.

Independence Day barbecue

Throw a few sprigs of rosemary on the barbecue coals while grilling veal or pork chops—the fragrance and flavor are delightful. Serve with boiled or steamed new carrots, sugar snap peas, and potato-and-onion cakes. To make the onion cakes, mix 3 cups cooked diced potatoes with 1 chopped onion, 2 eggs, 1¼ cups whipped cream, and season with salt, pepper, and nutmeg.

Divide the mixture between greased individual soufflé dishes and stand in a roasting pan half-filled with water. Bake in a preheated oven at 300°F for 1 hour. Leave to rest for 15 minutes before unmolding.

1

2

3

Hold thin red, white, and blue ribbons together and tie in a bow around rolled white napkins.

4

Independence Day

Make a simple table center of red, white, and blue flowers to complement a perfect white cloth.

Strawberries and cream extravaganza

Don't despair if you have to plan for unexpected guests, or something goes wrong with your dessert. You can create a fabulous dessert with the simplest of ingredients. A plain sponge cake doused with brandy or a strawberry mousse can be smothered with whipped cream mixed with a little confectioners' sugar then scattered with flaked almonds and decorated with halved strawberries. A fresh flower decoration completes the effect.

Yellow roses of Texas

Trim the rose blooms very close to the top and half-fill a wide, shallow glass bowl with water. Float a few blooms on the water and arrange one bloom next to the bowl.

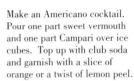

Make an Americano cocktail. Pour one part sweet vermouth and one part Campari over ice cubes. Top up with club soda and garnish with a slice of orange or a twist of lemon peel.

5

6

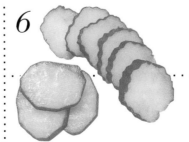

7

Boil new potatoes with half a raw beet then slice them to garnish meats or salads.

French-style sole roulade

6 sole fillets
12 thin slices Canadian bacon
salt and freshly ground
    black pepper
6 heads endive
3 tbsp butter
1½ cups heavy cream
dill sprigs

Flatten the sole fillets. Cut the bacon slices to fit them exactly, saving the trimmings. Season with salt and pepper and roll up neatly. Wrap tightly in plastic wrap and steam for 10 minutes.

Meanwhile, slice the chicory into fine julienne strips. Heat the butter until foaming and fry the chicory for 3 minutes, seasoning with salt and pepper. In a separate pan, bring the cream to boiling then blend with the chopped bacon trimmings. Spoon a little sauce on to a warmed serving plate and top with endive. Slice the sole roulade on top and garnish with dill.

8

A vital factor in ensuring success at a dinner party is to serve high quality wines.

9

Shape equal amounts of grated and cream cheese into a cylinder, roll in cracked peppercorns, slice, and serve on crackers.

10

Welcome your guests with a striking decoration of fresh or silk flowers in your theme colors at the bottom of the stairs.

Snowpeas with lemon sauce

Serve snowpeas lightly steamed as a vegetable, or refreshed in iced water for dipping. Either way, they are delicious with this lemon sauce.

2 egg yolks
3 tbsp French mustard
4 tbsp anchovies
juice of 1 lemon
1 shallot, chopped
1 cup oil
4 tbsp sour cream
    (optional)
salt and freshly ground
    black pepper

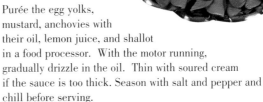

Purée the egg yolks, mustard, anchovies with their oil, lemon juice, and shallot in a food processor. With the motor running, gradually drizzle in the oil. Thin with soured cream if the sauce is too thick. Season with salt and pepper and chill before serving.

Fleur-de-lis napkins

Fold a napkin in half diagonally then bring the top corner down so that the point overlaps the folded edge. Turn over and repeat. Fold the napkin in concertina folds then arrange it in a glass, bending the sides downward. Pull the front layer of the napkin down over the glass.

11	*The French serve cheese before switching to a dessert or French vermouth with dessert.*	12
13		14 **Bastille Day**

Fruit and flower ice bowls

Ice bowls with flowers, herbs, fruit, or shells frozen into them make wonderful containers for ice creams, sorbets, and fruit salads. You will need two freezer-proof bowls, one slightly smaller. Fill the large bowl with 1¼ in of water. Place the smaller bowl centrally inside, position with tape and freeze until solid. Add more cold water until the remaining space is half-full, push in the decorations and freeze again. Fill with water and freeze again. Twist off the bowls by dipping in warm water for a few seconds.

Flower coasters

From a craft store, buy mother-of-pearl or cork disks slightly larger than the base of your glasses. Glue overlapping honesty seed cases round the edge and top with flower heads.

15

16

17

18

To make crushed ice, wrap ice cubes in a kitchen towel, and crush with a rolling pin.

For Marmalade cocktail, pour a measure of curaçao into an ice-filled glass, fill with tonic water and garnish with a kumquat "flower" or slice of orange.

Cocktail canapés

All these cocktail canapés are delicious—but simplicity itself to prepare.

Slice the top off kumquats and pipe on a swirl of cream cheese. Layer slices of ham with a mixture of cream cheese, a little horseradish sauce, and soured cream. Freeze until firm then cut into squares. Make choux pastry buns and fill with a mixture of mayonnaise, flaked salmon, and a little dill. Fill celery sticks with smoked salmon or light pâté and sprinkle with chives. Fill individual pastry cases with fried onions, beaten egg, and cream before baking. Slightly hollow out cherry tomatoes and pipe in a little cream cheese and chives. Wrap steamed asparagus in slices of prosciutto crudo. Spoon mayonnaise flavored with lemon juice and grated lemon rind into pastry cases and top with shrimp.

19

Wipe the rim of cocktail glasses with lemon juice or egg white then dip in colored sugar, shredded coconut or coffee granules.

20

21

Make a cocktail menu card and offer your guests a specific selection of cocktails.

Celebration strawberry gâteau

3 eggs
3 tbsp superfine sugar
6 tbsp all-purpose flour
pinch of salt
4 cups strawberries
6 tbsp strawberry jam
1¼ cups whipped
cream

Place the eggs in a mixing bowl
over a pan of simmering water
and gradually whisk in the sugar.
Whisk until pale and thick then
fold in the flour and salt. Divide
the mixture between 2 greased
7-in cake pans and bake in a
preheated oven at 300°F
for 15 minutes until golden
and springy. Leave to cool.
Rub half the strawberries
through a sieve then stir over a
gentle heat with sugar to taste until
the sugar has dissolved. Sandwich the cakes
together with jam and half the cream and pipe cream
round the top. Arrange the reserved strawberries in the
center and pour the purée over them.

22

23

Simple foods are often best for a
family occasion when you have
to cater for all ages.

24

Top iced cola in a tall glass
with a scoop of ice cream and
garnish with cocktail cherries.

25

Chicken and ham mushrooms

8 large mushrooms
1/3 cup cooked chicken, ground
1 slice cooked ham, chopped
1 egg, separated
2 green onions (scallions), sliced
salt and freshly ground black pepper
1/2 cup white wine
1/4 tsp cornstarch
2 tbsp sour cream
paprika

Chop the mushroom stalks, mix with the chicken, ham, egg yolk, and onions, and season with salt and pepper. Beat the egg white until stiff and fold in. Arrange the mushroom caps in a large saucepan, top with the mixture and surround with the wine. Cover and simmer for 5 minutes until tender. Transfer the mushrooms to a serving platter. Boil until the juices have reduced slightly. Stir in the cornstarch and cream and heat through gently. Spoon a little cream on each mushroom and sprinkle with paprika.

Sweet peas fill a glass jug and scent the whole room with their fragrance.

26

27

28

Snip wafer-thin lengthwise slices of zucchini like a comb, roll up and secure with a cocktail stick.

Triple-decker toasties

Fun to make and delicious to eat, this gives new meaning to the
old sandwich. Use toasted bread or different kinds of bread and
fill with layers of cheese, tomato, salmon, lettuce, ham, watercress, sliced gherkin, cold meats, or anything else you fancy.
A water melon makes a thirst-quenching end to a tasty meal.

Portable party rosettes

Cut a 22 x 3 in strip of
tissue paper, fold in small
concertina folds and staple one
end together. Tape two narrow strips
of card to the fan, open out, and
push the card strips into
a straw to hold the
fan open.

29

30

*Wieners topped up with boiling
water in a vacuum flask are
fun to take on your picnic.*

31

*Cool-bags are perfect for picnics.
Remember to freeze the blocks
the night before.*

Picnic fare

Don't just settle for cheese and pickle sandwiches if you are entertaining guests to a picnic. There are plenty of lovely recipes which will happily travel to the park as well as any sandwich! Fill French loaves with crisp salad leaves, cheese, and sliced meats. Take Scotch eggs (Apr 8), chicken coated in crispy bread crumbs, or ham and pepper omelet. Cornish pasties were designed as the perfect portable lunch. The originals even had a savory filling at one end and sweet at the other.

Quiches of all kinds are just right,
and take along some extra bread and butter,
drinks, a little salad, and some fresh fruit to finish.
Napkins, and knives for cutting the food, are also a must.

Guest list

Shrimp and balls of avocado, chunks of melon, cheese, or fig with raw ham, rolls of smoked ham or salami can all be speared on cocktail sticks for a tasty bite.

August

The lovely month of August is when you want to make the most of entertaining out-of-doors. Save your formal dinners for colder evenings and opt for a relaxed atmosphere with close friends, good wine, delicious food, and conversation among the flowers.

A summer wedding

A wedding reception held in a marquee is a great opportunity to create magnificent flower arrangements. A large tent really needs an impressive arrangement, and a pedestal is an ideal way to display the flowers to best advantage. Graceful little table decorations are given height by the miniature pedestal containers so they are raised above the food on the buffet tables.

The theme of pink-and-white runs through all these arrangements, but they still encompass a great many flowers from roses and gypsophila to daisies, carnations, and foxgloves.

Make a Honeymoon cocktail by shaking one part Benedictine, one part Calvados, one part lemon juice, and three dashes of orange curaçao.

1

2

Throw traditional rice instead of confetti, or choose confetti which the birds will eat.

3

Limit your buffet choices so that guests can try one of almost everything.

4

Salmon centerpiece

1 large salmon or salmon trout
1 lemon, sliced
2 bayleaves
3 parsley sprigs
1 cucumber, sliced
4 cups shrimp

Place a few slices of lemon, the bayleaves, and a little parsley on and inside the fish, wrap loosely in buttered foil and place on a cookie sheet. Bake in a preheated oven at 300°F for about 50 minutes until the skin loosens. Leave to cool in the foil. Remove the skin and lift off the top fillets. Remove the bones and replace the fillets. Garnish with cucumber, shrimp, lemon, and parsley.

Decorate your champagne

Using a plastic, cane, or wire ring which fits over the bottle, attach fresh flower heads all round the ring using florists' wire. Roses are always romantic, or you can echo the flowers used in the bride's bouquet.

5

Hollow out chunks of carrot or cucumber into boats and fill with mixed julienne vegetables.

6

7

Party rockets

As party gifts or unusual place markers, these silver rockets will really take off at any children's party. Use them as party bags at the end of the afternoon. Fold a square of silver paper in half in both directions, unfolding flat each time. Turn the paper over and fold diagonally. Open out, fold on the other diagonal, and leave folded. Hold the fold and push down so the front flap folds to the right and the back flap to the left. Fold the outer edges of the front flaps to the center, turn and repeat. Fold the outer corners of the front flaps to the center, turn and repeat. Fold the bottom points out. Gently open the rocket.

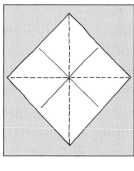
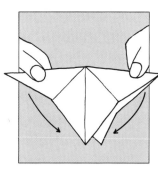
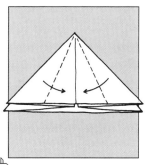
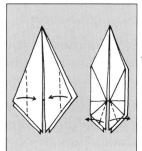

8

Provide some paper plates and colors and have the children decorate masks to take home.

9

10

11

Involve the children in the preparations for their party— they may have some great ideas.

A mega-burger party

Mexican topping:
1 avocado, mashed
1 clove garlic, crushed
2 tsp lemon juice
1 tomato, skinned and
  chopped

Blue cheese topping:
1 tbsp catsup
5 tbsp mayonnaise
6 tbsp sour cream

Tomato topping:
1¾ cups pure tomato juice
1 clove garlic, minced
2 tbsp chopped fresh
  tarragon
1 tbsp tarragon vinegar
pinch of sugar
2 tbsp oil

Mix together 2 lb ground beef, 1 minced onion, 4 tbsp Worcestershire sauce, and salt and pepper. To make burger fillings, combine ½ cup shredded Monterey Jack cheese with a chopped chili pepper; ½ cup blue cheese with 2 tbsp chopped walnuts; ½ cup Swiss cheese with ¼ cup chopped mushrooms. Carefully shape the meat into patties round each of the fillings and broil until cooked through. Mix the topping ingredients. Serve the burgers on warm rolls, spooning on the appropriate topping to taste.

Make some plain or chocolate roll-out cookies and cut them out with fancy cutters.

With a tube of gel or piped icing, decorate with ribbons and bows to look like little gifts.

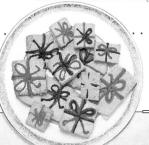

August

Outdoor breakfast

A continental breakfast is just asking to be served outdoors if you have guests during the summer. Decorate the table with a sunny little arrangement of marigolds and nasturtiums, and serve croissants with chilled butter and orange juice with some fresh fruit and freshly-made hot coffee.

Lady's slipper napkins

Quarter the napkin then fold it in half diagonally. Fold the sides so that they meet in the center. Turn the napkin over, fold up the flaps at the base then fold the napkin in half lengthwise. Turn over again and pull the loose corners upwards.

15	16
A substantial breakfast is better served as a brunch slightly later in the morning.	
17	18
	Bowls of fresh, fragrant rose petals make an original and delightful table centerpiece.

A formal breakfast

Formal breakfasts are a rarity these days, but it is fun to serve a traditional spread as brunch to friends staying for the weekend.

On the menu are: grapefruit, granola, croissants, rolls, soft-boiled eggs, hot toast, butter and marmalade, hash browns, pancakes, scrambled egg, and grilled or fried bacon, mushrooms, tomatoes, and sausages. To make corned beef hash, fry some chopped onion and bacon in oil until soft. Mix in 1 cup corned beef, 1½ cups mashed potato, 1 tbsp minced fresh parsley, and salt and pepper and fry until browned. To make kedgeree, mix 1 lb cooked, flaked smoked fish, ¾ cup cooked long-grain rice, ¼ cup butter, 2 chopped hard-cooked eggs, 2 tbsp chopped fresh parsley, ⅔ cup heavy cream and season with nutmeg, cayenne, salt, and pepper. Bake in a moderate oven for 30 minutes, stirring occasionally.

A healthy breakfast on a tray looks even more appetizing with a pretty posy of flowers alongside.

19

20

21

The perfect breakfast celebration drink is Buck's Fizz—champagne and fresh orange juice.

Silver anniversary trout

4 trout
2 tbsp all-purpose flour
salt and freshly ground black pepper
½ cup butter
juice of 1 lemon
2 tbsp minced fresh herbs such as parsley, chervil, tarragon
1 lemon, cut into wedges

Dust the trout with flour and season with salt and pepper. Heat half the butter until foaming then fry the trout on a fairly high heat for about 8 minutes per side. Transfer to a warmed serving platter and keep warm. Wipe out the pan and add the remaining butter. Cook until beginning to brown then add the lemon juice and herbs. Pour over the trout and serve with lemon wedges.

Frosted flowers

Beat an egg white until almost frothy and paint it all over flower heads such as sweet peas or roses. Transfer the flowers to wax paper coated with superfine sugar and dredge with more sugar. Shake off any excess then leave to dry.

22

23

24

Paper lace can be sprayed with silver to act as attractive place mats and coasters.

Silver for the table

A ring of evergreen surrounds a group of floating candles and pretty silver decorations to make this lovely anniversary table center. Use a wire or twig ring which will just surround a shallow bowl. Collect three or four different evergreen leaves, avoiding leaves which are too large, and wire them into the ring, making sure that it is completely covered.

Float the candles in the bowl, or line the bowl with silver foil and stand nightlights in it. Surround them with Christmas decorations or silver-sprayed fir cones.

Embroider a personal card for the anniversary couple, incorporating some of their main interests into the picture.

25	*Make place cards from silver card and decorate them with sequins.*	26	
27		28	*Stunning simplicity: a white-iced cake with blue icing flowers surrounded by sprays of curled silver ribbons.*

Barbecue parties

Position your main table to make the best of the floral displays in the garden, and enhance them with some simple table arrangements. Lighter colored flowers show up best in the evening, and chunky containers—pottery, earthenware, or basketware—suit the style of garden entertaining. For an interesting display, throw a Mexican blanket over a wheelbarrow and fill it with pots of flowers from inside or outside.

Offer a choice of wines, beers, and soft drinks to your guests. If it is a hot evening—or if the food is spicy—they will need more than usual to quench their thirsts. Provide plenty of places to sit and tables on which to eat, if possible. If you expect everyone to stand, plan your menu accordingly.

Choose colorful and edible flowers such as borage to freeze in ice cubes for summer drinks. Half-fill the ice cube mold, add the flower, and a little more water. Freeze, then top up and freeze again as the flowers float to the top.

29

Set up a canopy over your barbecue in case the weather takes a turn for the worse.

30

31

Always have more glasses than you think you need as people tend to use more than one.

A feast of fish

Be imaginative in your choice of fish for the barbecue. Here you can see red snapper and silver sardines striped with coarse-grained mustard. The trout are stuffed with chopped bacon, pine nuts, bread crumbs, and chives bound with cream; and the snapper with cooked rice, chopped peppers, fresh herbs, and shrimp. Kabobs combine monkfish, lemon, and zucchini brushed with oil and lemon juice and garnished with dill; or jumbo shrimp, scallops, and lime. Buttered corn provides the perfect accompaniment.

Adventurous barbecue salads can still be simple. Try flat-leaved parsley, tomatoes, and olives in French dressing, sprinkled with freshly grated Parmesan.

Garnish simply-barbecued mackerel with pats of chilled herb butter.

Guest list

September

*N*ow it is chillier in the evenings, it is back to
entertaining indoors—long, delightful evenings over
splendid dinners, planned and executed to perfection.
If you are well organized, you will be thinking about
preparations for the festive season!

Harvest supper

A table centerpiece for a harvest supper is just asking to combine fruits and flowers in the colors of the harvest: yellow, russet, and orange. Echo the richness of the theme in choosing wooden bowls and candle holders, and spread the arrangement loosely across the table for everyone's enjoyment. Keep the main flowers fresh by using a small bowl of florists' foam hidden by the fruit. Avoid making the arrangement too high, otherwise you will restrict people's view of the other guests and make conversation difficult. Make sure the flowers are only subtly fragrant, otherwise they may clash with the food.

Harvest tree

Use a ball of dry foam on a twig stem set among moss as the base for a waxed fruit table centerpiece. Wire the fruit carefully and arrange it in the foam until all the space is covered.

1   *A basket of fresh fruit, beautifully arranged, makes a lovely harvest table center.*   *2*

3   *4*   *Hitch up the edges of the table-cloth into scallops and decorate with posies of dried flowers.*

Cheese and wine

It has become popular recently to offer a wide selection of cheeses to guests after a meal. Naturally this means that almost everyone can enjoy their favorite cheese, but it also causes a few problems. The hostess will almost certainly be left with more cheese than she can use up while it is at its best. Also, different cheeses taste better with different wines, and a poor combination may spoil the enjoyment of one or other. Try buying just one or two excellent quality cheeses to serve with a complementary wine so that both can give of their best.

Wire tiny dried flower heads or fir cones together into a little posy and glue or wire them to cane or wooden rings to make charming napkin rings.

5

6   *Add a dash of grenadine and lemon juice to some apple juice and top up with ginger ale for a Rosy Pippin mocktail.*

7

Fondue party

A fondue party is a fun, informal way of entertaining your friends to a meal. Choose excellent quality meats and remove all trace of fat when you cut it into cubes. You can marinate it in oil and wine beforehand to ensure tenderness.

Offer plenty of fresh green salad to accompany the meat, and some hot baked potatoes in their jackets. Choose a selection of sauces so there is plenty of variety for your guests to try: curry or garlic mayonnaise, sour cream and chives, mustard, mushroom, chili or horseradish sauce.

Half-fill the fondue pot with oil and heat until a cube of bread will brown in less than a minute. Provide the guests with long-handled fondue forks so that they can cook their own meat.

Grand Marnier strawberry fondue

8 cups strawberries
6 squares milk chocolate, grated
6 squares plain chocolate, grated
1 cup heavy cream
3 tbsp Grand Marnier

To make a decorative stand, cover a dry foam cone with silver foil then layers of net. Cover the cone with strawberries fixed on with cocktail sticks. To make the sauce, melt the chocolate then add the cream. Stir in the liqueur and keep warm on a fondue stand.

8

9

Remember that meat or cheese fondues are very rich so accompanying salads should be crisp with a slight bite.

10

Always provide plenty of serving cutlery and plates on which to rest fondue forks.

11

Swiss cheese fondue

Swiss cheeses are ideal for cheese fondue. Add white wine, kirsch and garlic to the sauce. Serve breaded mushrooms, cubed bread, and crunchy vegetables. Potato balls are also very tasty. Mix mashed potato with egg yolk and a little flour, shape into small balls, coat in egg yolk, and roll in bread crumbs. Deep fry until golden brown.

Roll or fold beautiful lace or embroidered napkins to show them off to best advantage. Tie a bow of wide ribbon around the napkins and decorate with a flower or tiny pine cones.

Lemon baskets

Cut a lemon almost in half horizontally, then cut down at right angles and remove a wedge of fruit. Repeat on the other side, making a basket. Scoop out the flesh and fill the basket with fruits, sliced cucumber, herbs, or vegetable flowers.

12

13

14

Guests tend to eat more when they are cooking and eating in a leisurely atmosphere.

Entertaining Greek-style

2 tbsp olive oil
1 tbsp lemon juice
salt and freshly ground
    black pepper
1 clove garlic, crushed
1 zomaine lettuce, shredded
3 tomatoes, sliced
1/3 cup black olives,
    pitted
1/2 cup feta cheese,
    diced
1/2 red chili pepper,
    sliced
6 peperonata sausages
chopped fresh oregano

Whisk the oil, lemon juice, salt, pepper, and garlic until well emulsified. Place the lettuce on the bottom of a serving dish and arrange the other ingredients on top. Spoon over the dressing and sprinkle with oregano.

Choose a simple starter of crusty bread, butter, a selection of olives, and some tasty anchovies.

15

Save some old china and end your meal in the smashing Greek tradition!

16

17

18

Serve chilled ouzo in tall glasses with plenty of iced water.

Grilled sea bream

2 large sea bream
salt and freshly ground
    black pepper
2 lemons
2 thyme sprigs
2 oregano sprigs
3 tbsp olive oil
grape leaves

Sprinkle the fish inside and out with salt, pepper, and a little
lemon juice and place the herbs inside. Slash the sides and
sprinkle with lemon juice and oil. Broil for 20 minutes until
golden brown. Rinse preserved grape leaves or pour boiling water
over fresh grape leaves and stand
for 10 minutes. Drain and
arrange on a warmed serving
plate. Place the fish on top
and garnish with lemon
wedges.

Blue and white ribbons

Cover a cake pan with white
paper and stick strips of blue
florists' ribbon round the
outside. Fill the pan with
dry foam and arrange
blue and white
flowers in a
dome shape.
Fill the
spaces with
curls of blue
and white ribbon.

19

*If you can't make your own
baklava, buy it from the local
deli or a Middle Eastern
gourmet store.*

20

21

Harvest picnic

For a fall picnic select a coarse and a fine pâté and some strong cheese to serve with crusty breads and pickled onions. Serve some robust wines, preferably ones which do not need to be chilled, and crisp apples.

For a tasty chicken pâté, melt ¼ cup butter and sauté 1 cup trimmed chicken livers and a crushed garlic clove for 5 minutes, seasoning with salt and pepper. Purée, then add ½ cup melted butter, 2 tbsp dark sherry, and 1 tsp chopped fresh thyme. Press into ramekins and garnish with bayleaves.

Soak peeled pickling onions in salted water for 12 hours. Drain, rinse and pat dry then pack into jars and cover with pickling vinegar. Seal and store for at least 1 month.

Apple pomander

Pin two strips of narrow adhesive tape round a cooking apple. Stud with cloves, piercing the skin with a cocktail stick. Place 1 tsp each cinnamon and orris root powder in a paper bag and shake the apple in the bag. Seal and leave for 2 weeks. Remove the tape and decorate with ribbon.

Try serving a curried apple soup from a wide-mouthed flask with crusty bread.

22

23

24

Apples and cheese are the perfect snack partners for a selection of tangy and unusual pickles.

25

26

A rich, dry alcoholic cider is a traditional choice for a fall picnic.

27

A pot of baby wipes will come in useful at a picnic for wiping or mopping.

28

Sloe gin for Christmas

1 cup ripe sloes
4-6 oz sugar
3 cups gin

Remove the stalks from the sloes and wash them well. Prick them at both ends and put them into a screw-top or Mason jar which should be no more than half full. Add sugar to taste and top up with gin. Seal the container and shake vigorously. Shake the jar twice daily for four weeks, then leave to mature for as long as possible. The liquid can be strained and bottled after 3 months.

29

Make mincemeat, cakes, and puddings now so they can mature in time for Christmas.

30

Guest list

Chocolate mousse

6 squares semi-sweet
    chocolate, chopped
5 tbsp water
1 tbsp butter
2 tbsp rum
3 eggs, separated

Melt the chocolate with
the water in a bowl over
a pan of hot water.
Remove from the heat
and beat in the butter.
Add the rum and gradually beat in the
egg yolks. Whisk the egg whites until stiff but not
dry and fold them into the
chocolate. Spoon into glasses
and chill overnight.
Garnish with whipped
cream and chocolate.

*Budget for entertaining at
Christmas by buying a few extra
items each week during the fall.*

Place sprigs of fresh tarragon
and a piece of lemon rind in
bottles of white wine vinegar.
Seal and leave for two weeks
before using.

Blossoming candles

Mark the size of a candle in a
block of dry foam, cut a ring of
foam to fit round the candle
then place it in the holder. Cut
ferns or greenery and arrange
round the ring. Cut flower
stems quite short and press
between the greenery until the
ring is completely covered.

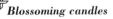

This season of mellow fruitfulness is wonderful for entertaining, creating just the right atmosphere for cozy suppers with friends or splendid formal dinners. Whichever you prefer, make your October entertaining stylish.

1

2

Lighting for a dinner party should be soft and relaxing but not too dim.

3

Boil 1¾ cups sugar with 6 tbsp water to a golden caramel and use to coat pairs of grapes.

4

Formal dinner party

Two or four guests is ideal for a small formal dinner party so that the conversation does not split into smaller groups. Your invitations will have set the tone for the occasion, so your guests will expect something special. Don't let the table disappoint them—it is the focus of the evening and worth the thought and effort which will need to go into its preparation. Choose a low floral table centerpiece and provide candlelight or subtle lighting. Display your best china, silverware, and glassware with crisp white linen, spotlessly clean and starched. A beautifully written menu card and matching place cards will show your guests exactly what treats are in store for them.

Look out for unusual containers in which to place small floral arrangements on your table or sideboard.

Chocolate leaf dessert

½ cup unsalted butter
10 squares semi-sweet chocolate
3 eggs, separated
¼ cup superfine sugar
1 tbsp all-purpose flour
¼ cup ground almonds
1 tsp vanilla extract
3 cups chocolate chips

Cut place cards from white or colored card. Glue a small arrangement of pressed flowers in one corner. Write the guest's name and cover the card with plastic wrap.

Beat half the butter then beat in 4 squares softened chocolate. Add the egg yolks one at a time. Fold in the sugar, flour, almonds, and vanilla extract. Beat the egg whites and fold in. Pour into a greased cake pan and bake in a preheated oven at 350°F for 45 minutes. Cool then slice horizontally into 3 layers. Melt the remaining chocolate and butter. Use to sandwich the layers together and cover the cake. Melt the chocolate chips and spread thinly on to wax paper. When cold, peel away the paper and cover the cake with the sheets of chocolate.

5

6

7

Nothing can compare with the beauty of cut glass for a formal dinner table.

Harlequin scallops

54 scallops
2 tbsp olive oil
1 clove garlic, chopped
1 red bell pepper, cubed
1 green bell pepper, cubed
1 stick celery, cubed
2 carrots, cubed
pinch of thyme
salt and freshly
*   ground black pepper*
Scallop or other shells

Arrange the scallops on a plate. Heat the oil and garlic, add all the ingredients and fry gently for about 10 minutes, stirring, until tender but still crisp. Fill the shells with the mixture and place in a hot oven for a few minutes to heat through completely.

Elegant napkins

Fold the napkin lengthwise into three. With the loose edge away from you, fold the short edges in to meet in the center. Fold down the top corners to meet in the center. Turn over. Lift and tuck one side into the other then turn again as illustrated.

8

9

Part-baked fancy breads save time and can be served hot from the oven.

10

Mincemeat-stuffed apples drizzled with brandy and brown sugar make a tasty fall dessert.

11

If you are short of flowers, use a pretty flowering pot plant in an attractive container as a table centerpiece.

Ornamental centerpiece

A decorative pink and green ornamental cabbage can make a wonderful table centerpiece. As it has to last only a short time, the flowers are simply placed among the leaves. Remove any damaged or dirty outside leaves from the cabbage and cut off the base so that the cabbage will stand securely. Arrange it on a flat plate or mat. Cut the stems of the flowers quite short and tuck them in between the layers of leaves until you have a pleasing arrangement.

12

13

14

Cut ears and a mouth, add clove eyes and cocktail stick legs to make a lemon pig.

Winter wedding

The wedding cake is often the centerpiece of the wedding breakfast so the cake you choose should reflect the style of your wedding. Commercially-made cakes can be exquisite, or you or a friend may be able to decorate an ornate cake. But if these options are not available, you can still produce a splendid cake.

Make up three rich fruit cakes in round or square pans. Cut the surfaces smooth then turn the cakes upside-down so that you have completely flat tops. Cover with almond paste then roll-out frosting. This cake has been tinted a subtle peach to match the bridal color scheme. A little royal icing piped round the bases of the cakes is simple, and a garland of lace and posies of silk flowers complete the picture.

Make lacy place cards for your top table by sticking some lace around colored card and decorating with pressed flowers.

Children will be both seen and heard—deputize someone to entertain them.

15

16

17

18

Table centerpieces

It can be expensive to produce large numbers of table centers for a wedding reception. Mold chicken wire into low bowls to support the flowers, then use flourishes of inexpensive flowers or greenery dotted with contrasting blooms.

Ceviche appetizer

For Cod Ceviche, season and marinate 12 oz cubed cod in ¼ pt lime juice with 1 tsp paprika and ½ small chopped onion for at least 3 hours.

To make Oyster Ceviche, marinate 24 oysters in ¼ pt lime juice for 6 hours, season and add 1 tbsp tomato pulp, 1 chopped onion, and 1 tbsp chopped mint. Drain off excess liquid.

Shrimp Ceviche is made by marinating 3 cups cooked peeled shrimp in ⅔ cup lime juice with the juice of 1 orange for at least 3 hours. Stir in ½ chopped onion, 1 tbsp tomato pulp, 1 chopped chili, 1 tbsp oil, ½ tsp Worcestershire sauce, and a few drops of Tabasco sauce.

19

20

Your seating plan should sit guests with other people with similar interests.

21

Wrap candies in colored net and tie with ribbon to make little children's gifts.

Smørrebrød

Despite much confusion outside Scandinavia, smörgåsbord and smørrebrød are not the same. The latter is Danish open sandwiches rather than the Swedish buffet. Use a selection of breads for your sandwiches, including different rye breads.

Favorite toppings include salami, cream cheese, cheese, ham, tongue, herrings, or hard-cooked eggs artfully garnished with tomatoes, gherkins, onion rings, bacon strips, olives, or anchovies and displayed on a bed of lettuce or on wooden boards.

Push a skewer through a 4-in piece of cucumber. Slice through to the skewer at a slight angle, turning and cutting into a spiral.

22

Pickle fans and sliced beets with onions go well with this style of buffet.

23

24

25

Schnapps is traditional with smörgåsbord, although it may be too fiery for some guests so offer alternatives.

Smörgåsbord

A Scandinavian smörgåsbord is an unusual way to present a themed buffet. Offer a selection of cold meats and Scandinavian cheeses garnished with dill, red onions, and capers. A large bowl of fresh fruit can provide a tasty centerpiece. Salads should feature beets, onion, and sugar-sprinkled cucumber in white wine vinegar. Soused herrings and other marinated fish are deliciously different. Try your own recipes or buy a few varieties from the supermarket. A rich pork terrine is often a feature of a smörgåsbord. If you line the pan with stretched bacon strips before you add the terrine mixture, the effect is particularly attractive. Hot dishes are also often served, such as spiced meatballs or chopped wieners in a hot potato salad.

Scandinavian paper houses

Cut a shape out of colored paper based on a 2-in base with sides 4 in high. Stick on cut-out windows and a door and colored shapes on the roof. Fold and glue together and fix a small paper handle. Fill with sweets or a gift for each guest.

Complete your meal in Scandinavian style by serving a selection of Danish pastries.

Halloween lantern

A pumpkin lantern is the highlight of the Halloween party but is very simple to make from any size of pumpkin. Slice off and reserve the top. Using a sharp spoon, scoop out the flesh to use for a delicious pumpkin soup. Scrape away until you have a thick, hollow bowl—also ideal for serving the soup! Draw a face on one side of the pumpkin then cut it out. Place a nightlight or candle inside and replace the lid. For a small lantern, you can fix some string on either side for carrying.

Echo the rich orange colors in your flower arrangements. Clusters of rose hips and berries can be mixed with chrysanthemums and helichrysums for a fabulous display.

Halloween cups

Using small balls from a craft store, glue on ghoulish paper faces and hats, and attach curled florists' ribbon for hair. Gently stretch strips of crepe paper to make capes to glue to the necks and fix the monsters over tall glasses.

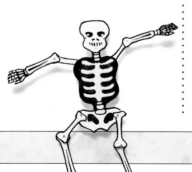

29

30

31

Halloween

Make paper skeletons to hang or sit at each place setting.

Witches' hats, spiders, and bats can all be cut out into stencils then sprayed in white on to black napkins or in black on spooky green.

Braided lamb

2 eggs, beaten
2 cups ground lamb
2 onions, chopped
2 tbsp bread crumbs
1 tsp dried rosemary
1 tbsp tomato paste
1 tbsp Worcestershire sauce
salt and freshly ground black pepper
8 oz puff pastry

Mix 1 egg with the filling ingredients. Roll out the pastry into a rectangle and place the lamb down the center. Cut diagonal strips from the center to the edges along both sides. Brush with egg and braid the strips over the lamb, meeting in the center. Brush with egg and cook in a preheated oven at 425°F for 20 minutes.

Guest list

Make large witches' hats or masks for your guests out of black paper.

*A*s fall moves into winter, November is the time for fun family gatherings and lighthearted entertaining. Don't let the cold get you down, let it inspire you to be more adventurous in your cooking and entertaining.

Hot apple pizza

1¼ cups whole-wheat flour
1 package active dry yeast
½ tsp ground cinnamon
2 tbsp butter
5 tbsp apple juice
2 red apples,
*   sliced*
2 tbsp raisins
2 tbsp hazel-
*   nuts*

Mix the flour,
cinnamon, and
1 tbsp butter.
Add 4 tbsp warmed
apple juice to the
yeast; leave to foam for
10 minutes. Mix with the
flour and make a dough and
knead well. Cover and
leave to rise for 15 minutes.
Press into a circle. Arrange
the apples on top, sprinkle
with raisins, hazelnuts, and
juice and dot with butter.
Bake in a preheated oven at
400°F for 20 minutes.

Mix 7½ cups
fresh tea, 2½ cups
brandy, 2½ cups dark rum,
and sugar to taste and heat
gently. Decorate with twists of
lemon and serve Hot Tea Punch
to your bonfire guests.

For a children's Halloween
party, you can't beat a plate of
hot beans and sausage links.

1

2

3

4

Halloween party rice soup

¼ cup brown rice
2 cups water
1 tbsp butter
2 onions, chopped
2 sticks celery, chopped
1 tsp dried thyme

3¾ cups vegetable
    broth
1 tbsp soy sauce
4 potatoes, diced
1 carrot, diced
2 tbsp heavy cream

Bring the rice and water to boiling and simmer for about 40 minutes until tender. Melt the butter and sauté the onions until soft. Add the celery and thyme and cook for 5 minutes. Add the remaining ingredients except the cream and simmer for 20 minutes until cooked. Purée then add the rice, stir in the cream and reheat gently.

Explosive arrangement

A fiery table centerpiece of purples and reds is a must for bonfire night. Arrange wire or dry foam in a shallow bowl and cover with greenery. Build up a display of tall-stemmed flowers radiating from the center.

5

Guy Fawkes Night

6

7

Diwali celebration

The Hindu festival of lights is celebrated in October or November. Choose the occasion to serve a classic Indian meal to your friends, such as this Chicken Chaat.

3 cloves garlic, minced
1 tsp salt
2 tbsp oil
1½ lb chicken, cubed
1½ tsp ground coriander
pinch of turmeric
½ tsp chili powder
1½ tbsp lemon juice
2 tbsp chopped fresh coriander
 (cilantro)

Crush the garlic and salt to a paste. Heat the oil and brown the garlic then add the chicken and fry for 8 minutes, stirring. Add the coriander, turmeric, and chili and fry for 5 minutes until the chicken is cooked. Stir in the lemon juice and chopped coriander and serve with lemon wedges and salad.

Purée a large can of mango pulp with 1¼ cups milk, 4 tbsp superfine sugar, and 1 tsp ground cardamom. Pour into a jug with 1¼ cups each milk and water and chill. Serve in a frosted glass.

8

Cut a diamond pattern on a half-mango and reverse the shape to make a hedgehog garnish.

9

10

11

Lager makes a refreshing drink to serve with highly-spiced Indian foods.

Festival of lights

Press several tall, thin, colored candles into a block of dry foam in a wide bowl. Wrap a swathe of kitchen foil around the edge to make a splendid and simple table centerpiece.

Candle fold napkins

Fold a napkin in half diagonally. Turn up the folded edge about 1¼ in then turn the napkin over. Roll the napkin into a cylinder and tuck in the end. Fold down the front corner.

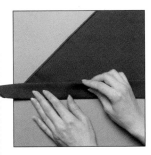

12

13

Deep-fry popadoms in a wire basket, pressing them into a cup for chutney or onion rings.

14

Buffet nouveau

In France, the third Thursday in November is when the first of the Beaujolais Nouveau becomes available—what a great excuse for inviting friends for a wine-tasting! Choose burgundy colors as your table theme, introducing some peach-colored flowers and a madras check cloth for variety and fun. A simple buffet will be enjoyed by your guests while they decide how they will judge this year's wines.

Use chives or a ring of carrot, onion or zucchini to tie up little bundles of blanched vegetable sticks as garnishes for meat or vegetable dishes.

Nouveau in November

Make a classy cover for your bottles of Nouveau by taping a strip of gold or fancy card into a cylinder. Cut the top edge with scissors or pinking shears. Attach a little bunch of grapes made from paper-covered chocolate candies glued together.

15

Roll puff pastry trimmings into little bunches of grapes as a garnish.

16

17

18

Store wine bottles on their sides in a room where there is little temperature variation.

Pears in red wine

2½ cups dry red wine
juice of ½ lemon
1 strip lemon rind
1 cup sugar
1 stick cinnamon
6 pears, peeled
1 tbsp flaked almonds

Bring the wine, juice, rind, sugar, and cinnamon to boiling, stirring until the sugar dissolves. Boil for 1 minute. Core the pears from underneath. Add to the pan and simmer for 20 minutes until just soft, basting. Leave to cool in the syrup then transfer to a serving dish and discard the cinnamon and rind. If the syrup is thin, stir in 1 tbsp arrowroot mixed with water and boil until thick and clear. Spoon over the pears and garnish with flaked almonds.

19

20

21

Most red wines are best served at room temperature and opened an hour before serving.

Thanksgiving celebration

Three simple white candles look stunning among this loose fall collection. A bed of moss and nuts surrounds a central core of dry foam in a shallow glass bowl. The candles are pressed in to the foam and surrounded by a varied arrangement of cinnamon sticks, dried flowers, twigs, and berries. Be adventurous in your choice of materials for an arrangement of this kind and experiment to see which give the best effects.

Envelope place cards

Make miniature envelopes out of wrapping paper or air mail paper, leaving the flap open. Glue a few pressed flowers as though they are emerging from the envelope and tie on a curl of florists' ribbon.

22

23

24

Little cane squirrel nut baskets make attractive place markers or gifts.

25

Thanksgiving

Serve rich, fruity Californian wine to celebrate Thanksgiving.

American corn cake

2½ cups milk
2 tbsp brown sugar
½ tsp vanilla extract
1¼ cups fine yellow cornmeal
2 eggs, separated
¼ cup butter
pinch of salt

Bring the milk, sugar, and
vanilla to boiling, then stir
in the cornmeal. Cool slightly.
Beat in the egg yolks and butter.
Beat the egg whites and salt until stiff.
Stir a spoonful of cornmeal into the
whites then fold them into the cornmeal.
Pour into a greased and lined 7-in
loose-bottomed cake pan
and bake in a preheated
oven at 350°F
for 40 minutes.

Make diagonal slices to cut
wedges out of a half-apple.
Cut the four inner wedges
in half crosswise then
reshape into
apple boats.

26

27

Glue popcorn to a dry foam ring
or circle of card and decorate
with ribbons as a fun table
decoration.

28

Sophisticated appetizers

"Caviar" does not have to be Beluga to make a wonderful appetiser served on a bowl of ice with sour cream and clarified butter. Make little pancakes to serve with the caviar by beating 1 cup all-purpose flour, 1 cup milk, 1 tbsp melted butter, 2 tsp sugar, pinch of salt, 2 eggs, and a splash of soda water until smooth and thick enough to coat the back of a spoon. Leave to rest for 2 hours. Fry spoonfuls in a little butter for about 3 minutes each side until golden brown.

Venison with pears

Bring to boiling 1¼ cups each oil and wine vinegar, 2½ cups white wine, 1 bouquet garni, a few parsley stalks, rind of ½ orange, 8 crushed juniper berries, 1 sliced onion, 1 stick celery, 1 crushed clove garlic. Simmer for 5 minutes then cool, pour over a saddle of venison and marinate for 24 to 48 hours.

　　Drain the meat and rub with butter, salt, and pepper. Cover with foil and roast in a preheated oven at 375°F, basting. Uncover and cook for a further 1 hour. Add some halved pears, dotted with butter and cinnamon, to the pan 30 minutes before the end of cooking.

29

30　　　　　　St Andrew's Day

Finish your meal with a tot of fine Scottish malt whisky served with coffee.

Cross a plain white tablecloth diagonally with blue ribbons or crepe paper to celebrate St Andrew's Day.

Curried fruit

1 cup light brown sugar
⅔ cup white wine vinegar
⅔ cup water
4 cloves
2 tbsp curry powder
1 tsp coriander seeds
3 apples, peeled, cored, and sliced
¾ cup pineapple chunks
3 tbsp raisins
6 apricots, pitted and sliced

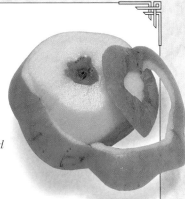

Mix the sugar, vinegar, water, and spices, bring to boiling and
simmer for 5 minutes. Add the apples, pineapple, and raisins
and simmer, uncovered, for about 10 minutes, stirring
frequently. Add the apricots and simmer for a further 10
minutes until the fruit is just soft and the sauce is thick. Bottle
in hot jars, seal, and cover.

Guest list

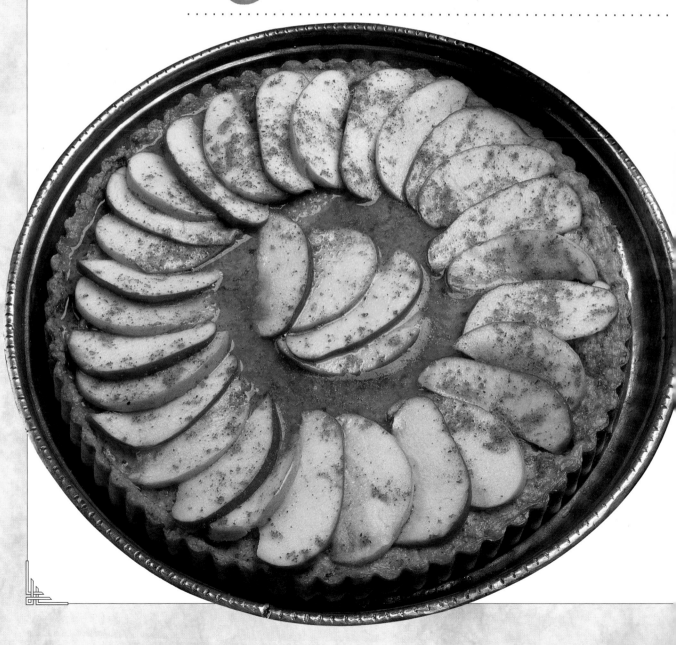

ecember—and everyone immediately thinks of entertaining at Christmas. Spend some time early in the month preparing for the festive season and your Christmas fare will be all the more admired.

December

Personalized Christmas Cards

Cut simple festive shapes—such as Santa Claus, a Christmas pudding, a little robin, or a Christmas tree—out of brightly colored felt and make individual Christmas cards or place cards for your guests. For really personalised cards, think of something specific such as their favorite hobby to incorporate into the design.

Glue onto contrasting fabric or colored card, and attach ribbons, sequins, or bows for a really three-dimensional effect.

Mix 6 tbsp chocolate spread and 2 tbsp hot water then mix in 1 cup cake crumbs and shape into balls. Decorate with white marzipan, licorice candies, and coconut to make snowmen and Christmas puddings.

1

2 Spray fir cones gold or silver and attach a matching place card with curls of silver florists' ribbon.

3 Add a tablespoon of sherry and a chopped apple to spice up store-bought mincemeat.

4

Pasta rings

Use a dry foam ring or smaller firm shape and glue on a mixture of dried pasta shapes. Cover the ring entirely and leave to dry. Spray completely in gold, then wrap round a bright red ribbon and tie in a bow.

5

6

7

Make seasonal petits fours with colored marzipan shaped as robins or puddings.

Unexpected guests

Keep your freezer well stocked to cope with unexpected guests. A couple of flans and some half-baked breads are always a useful standby. You can make a delicious store-cupboard salad with cooked pasta mixed with some sliced green onions (scallions), chopped mixed herbs, and drained cans of red kidney beans, quartered mushrooms, and flaked tuna.

Mix ⅔ cup olive oil, 3 tbsp white wine vinegar, 1 tbsp Dijon mustard, and a squeeze of lemon juice to dress the salad before serving with crusty bread.

8

9

Spray some bay or laurel leaves gold and glue round a dry foam or card ring for a simple table centerpiece.

10

Keep a bag of frozen sticks of cream in the freezer so you can defrost a small quantity as you need it.

11

Silk flowers

Silk flowers can be fairly expensive, but they are made to last, and a classic arrangement is a good investment if you like to keep a floral display around the house. They will always brighten up the home, and can be used as a ready-made table centerpiece when you have no time to prepare a more elaborate arrangement.

Mock Daisy Crusta: pour the juice of two limes and 1 tbsp raspberry syrup over crushed ice in a tall glass. Top up with soda water and float a little grenadine on top. Garnish with mint and raspberries on a stick.

12

13

14

Fry mixed nuts in hot oil, sprinkle with ginger, cinnamon, and cayenne, and brown under a hot broiler.

Mulled wine and mince pies

This is the classic Christmas fare to offer your neighbors when they come to wish you all the best for the festive season. If you do not have time to make your own mincemeat, choose a good quality commercial brand; there are plenty from which to select.

To make mulled wine, slice an orange, leaving the top slice very thick. Stud this with cloves and add to a pan with the orange slices, 2 bottles of red wine—nothing too special—1 cup brown sugar, 2 sticks cinnamon, and the rind of 1 lemon. Stir over a low heat until the sugar has dissolved then simmer for about 5 minutes. Add 1¼ cups brandy, if you wish, and serve in heatproof glasses.

A garland of nuts

Nuts are plentiful at Christmas and you can take advantage of their wonderful shapes and textures to make an attractive table center. Press into a dry foam ring or glue them round a wide cylinder of card with some fir cones, red and green Christmas baubles, and tartan bows. Even simpler, pile the arrangement into a shallow bowl—but expect it to disappear gradually over the vacation!

15	16
	Blend equal quantities of butter and sugar, and flavor with brandy and grated orange rind.
17	18
Decorate plainly-wrapped presents with simple, colorful Christmas shapes.	

MINI ANGEL COLLAR

MINI ANGEL WINGS
Cut 1 in white paper

MINI ANGEL ARMS
Cut 1 in white paper

MINI ANGEL PLACECARD
Cut 1 in white paper

MINI ANGEL PLACECARD
Cut 1 in gold card

MINI ANGEL DRESS
Cut 1 in white paper

MINI ANGEL HALO

JOSIE

LEYNA

JOHN

Angel place cards

Cut out the dress, arms, wings, and name card from thin white card. Decorate with gold thread and gold pen, and make hair in gold knitting yarn. Cut a little collar from paper lace and assemble the angel to wait at your table.

19

Pop a knob of brandy butter inside the lid of hot mince pies.

20

21

22	23	*Trim red and green chili peppers, slit almost to the base, and chill in iced water to make beautiful flower garnishes.*

24 **Christmas Eve**	25 **Christmas Day**
Disguise the Christmas tree tub with swathes of colored satin fabric remnants.	

Christmas Day

A glowing fire offers a traditional Christmas welcome, and this tree lavishly decked with baubles and swirls of ribbon is as inviting as the presents arranged temptingly underneath. If you do not have room for a large tree, stand a smaller one on a table and decorate it in style. You may like a sentimental range of decorations collected gradually over the years, or prefer a limited range of colors: red, green, and gold, or silver and pink, for example. Echo the colors by draping the table with a long and a short cloth in matching colors and hang little stockings round the edge of the table. Smother the tree with lights and it will give off a warm and welcoming glow.

Christmas tree boxes

Cut the shape from a piece of card in any size to fit your gift. Score and bend to create a pyramid shape and punch holes in the tops to thread with ribbon. Decorate to look like a Christmas tree, sticking on sequins, braid or gold paper.

Rich Christmas pudding

Mix 3 cups each all-purpose flour and bread crumbs, 6 cups raisins, 4 cups currants, ¼ cup mixed peel, 2¼ cups shredded suet, and 2 cups soft brown sugar. Add 4 beaten eggs, juice, and grated rind of an orange and a lemon, ½ tsp each salt, mixed spice, ginger, and nutmeg and 1½ cups Guinness. Cover and leave overnight. Press into 2 pudding basins, cover and steam for 8 hours. Steam for a further 2 hours before serving topped with holly and flamed with warm brandy.

Gold holly leaf shapes on red and green cards make festive place cards or gift tags.

New Year buffet

If you give a little extra thought to how you present your buffet table, even the simplest foods will look spectacular. This appetizer, attractive in itself, is turned into a really original and stunning table centerpiece for a buffet by using red cabbage leaves to cup the individual salads, contrasting with the sprigs of fresh watercress. Offer a range of salads to go with the meats or cheese dishes you have chosen, and remember that guests will be managing with just a fork, so avoid foods which are difficult to eat.

Ritz Fizz

Pour a dash each of Amaretto, blue curaçao, and clear lemon juice into a wine glass, top with chilled champagne, and garnish with a rose petal.

26

Always provide plenty of non-alcoholic drinks for those who are driving home.

27

28

29

Spread triangles of puff pastry with mustard, cover with a slice of cheese, ham or salami, roll and shape into crescents before baking in a hot oven for 10 minutes.

Party cones

Twist colored card into a cone shape, line with tissue paper and add a card handle. Fill with strips of colored tissue paper with some streamers, a blower, and a paper hat on top to give to guests just before midnight.

30

Guest list

31

New Year's Eve

Have a Happy New Year's entertaining!

Index